Blessing Over Darkness

Pheara (Peter) Am was born in the Capital of Phnom Penh, the Kingdom of Cambodia.

Am was at first working as Teacher Assistant/Librarian for Quaker Services Australia (QSA), later as an Interpreter/Translator for Forces Commander Office, a High Profile Environment of the United Nations, Then, Assistant Business Manager, Telstra OTC, Australian Telecommunication, Project Manager for Save the Children Norway, Cambodia Office and currently as a Banker, Wells Fargo Bank, N.A.

Am holds a Master of Business Administration (MBA) from the American InterContinental University in Houston, State of Texas, The United States of America.

Am married to his Beautiful wife, Romona.

Blessing Over Darkness

A Real Life Journey from Darkness to Blessing

Pheara (Peter) Am

iUniverse, Inc.
New York   Bloomington

Blessing Over Darkness
A Real Life Journey from Darkness to Blessing

iUniverse books may be ordered through booksellers or by contacting:

iUniverse
1663 Liberty Drive
Bloomington, IN 47403
www.iuniverse.com
1-800-Authors (1-800-288-4677)

Because of the dynamic nature of the Internet, any Web addresses or links contained in this book may have changed since publication and may no longer be valid. The views expressed in this work are solely those of the author and do not necessarily reflect the views of the publisher, and the publisher hereby disclaims any responsibility for them.

ISBN: 978-1-4401-2407-5 (pbk)
ISBN: 978-1-4401-2408-2 (ebk)

Printed in the United States of America

iUniverse rev. date: 3/24/2009

To My Family- Pa, Mak, sister Elizabeth, Margaret and brother Reagan
Who has given me wonderful life, love, encouragement, help, light and hope

To My beautiful, lovely and Godly wife, Romona who always give me
Guidance, direction and support especially happiness

Special thanks to my best friend Trishatur Lagalia, Professor Larry Smith,
Steve Bennett, family, friends and people who help me to make this book happen

My gratitude goes to Mr. Yamashita Junshi who gave me
A marvelous opportunity to have higher education
In the United States of America

Khmer Republic and the Government of Lon Nol
(1970 to 1975)
Phnom Penh – The Beginning of My Life

My name is Collacot and I was born in June 1970 in Phnom Penh, the capital of Cambodia. There were six members in our family: Mom, Dad, my older brother Reagan and my two sisters, oldest, Elizabeth and youngest, Margaret and me. We were lucky to have a home that everyone enjoyed living. My father was the Chief Bureau, Topography Department, The Ministry of Agriculture. My mother was a businesswoman.

In Cambodia, the way of life for people who live in the city and countryside was completely different. Because we lived in the city of Phnom Penh our family was considered middle-class. Most people who live in the city have basic need and countryside not. We even owned a French-made "Deux Chevaux" 2CV & all A model Citroen car. My Mom was a good-hearted person and would help feed her older sister's sons. My cousins, Ang and Sung, were from the countryside, Kampuchea Krom but they stayed with us. My aunt realized that if her sons were to have a good education they would have to live in the city.

In 1974, at the age of four I attended "Petit Lycee Bayon," a French kindergarten. I went to school four days a week, from Monday to Friday, except Thursdays. Each day I was picked up by the school bus around 6:30 am and dropped back home around 3:00 pm. I really enjoyed school and found it fun. There I learned to sing in Khmer and French. I also learned to read and write. There were times when I would cry because I didn't want to go to school.

On those days my cousins Ang and Sung would cheer me up by comforting me and giving me some toys and promising to take me around in the city for sightseeing along the river bank, national parks, children playground and Independent Monuments. They both continued asking me why I did not want to go to school. They said, there must be reasons behind. I told them about the reasons why I did not want to go to school.

I told him the story what was happening. I was afraid of someone in the school who is older than me that he might kick me. Cousins Ang and Sung asked me to listen to them. They taught me techniques on what and how to counter the situation and self-defense. He is asking me, will I be able to do it and put it into practices? I replied yes, yes to their questions and then he put me on the school bus, which was waiting for me.

At that time my brother Reagan and my eldest sister Elizabeth attended Santhor Mok School. They also enjoyed going to school. That same year my sister Elizabeth became seriously ill and passed away. My family held a funeral ceremony for her to ensure that her soul would rest in peace in heaven.

Once in a while my brother Reagan would takes me on "Lampata", a Cambodian three-wheeled taxi, light passenger mini-bus to see a movie. An usher would escort us to our seats in the theater. We mostly liked to see martial-arts movies. After the movie we would go sightseeing in the city. I felt so happy each time I went out with my brother. We always had such great fun! Phnom Penh was a very beautiful city with nice parks. Most of the buildings, apartments and houses in the city were built in the French colonial architectural style.

Cambodia had good system of clean roads that linked the major cities throughout the country. In every provincial town, you can see nice parks, schools, and universities with well maintenance. If you travel to Cambodia, you can see all the achievements, roads, power plants, clean water system and buildings, which was done by Sangkum Reas Niyum and the Khmer Republic.

Nearly every Sunday our family and relatives would gather for a picnic. Each family prepared everything needed before going there. With nice and clean road we all traveled by car to Bokor. Bokor is a resource close to the Capital of Phnom Penh. It was full of forest, pine trees, water fall from up hill to down hill with beautiful weather. King Sihanouk also had a palace on the top of Bokor hill where His Royal Highness and Her Majesty and Families stay on vacation.

We had barbeque beef on the stick, mixed vegetables pickle-salads, tomato, carrot, cucumbers, green pepper and ginger root with stem rice and soft drink. We sometimes had grill chicken and fish with cabbages pickle. After the dish, I like having fresh papaya, mango and pineapple.

My Mom, my Dad, uncles, cousins and we all enjoyed eating and playing during the picnic. The young and women go to the waterfall where men go to play volleyball, then back to the waterfall again. We saw not only our family but also all other people there were having a good time. This moment was the light of everyone's life and these thoughts is always in my mind.

My uncle Song had the largest family with six children. Here they were names her five girls: Ry, Reth, Roth, Tin, Pov and one boy: Pros. Uncle Son and his wife had one girl name Vy. Next was my aunt Sar and her husband with four children: her two sons, Lundy and Ra and her two daughters: Dovin and Vireak. Then there was aunt Sang with her two children Stella and Marakot. Finally, there were my two young unmarried uncles Kim Duth and Sokhak and aunt Sinh. During the time of the Khmer Republic my family and relatives lived happily and peacefully.

Whenever my aunts, uncles and cousins came to our house on Sunday they always talked about politics and the latest in Cambodian society. I was fortunate to be born at the time of the prosperous Khmer Republic time. My parents told me that Cambodia's standard of living during this time was very good. In fact, seventy-five percent of Cambodians in the Republic had all their basic needs met. Cambodia's economy, although small, was considered a strong one and our economy was often compared to that of our neighboring countries, Malaysia, Thailand and Singapore.

When I was very young, my parents, Aunts and uncles always tell me about communist and country's politics. They told me that communist is evil and how inhumanity they are. Listening to that story, I felt scaring and wondering in my mind, heart and soul that how, what and why can people kill or tyrannize the other. This memory was still in my mind.

During my childhood family gatherings I recall listening to the discussions about society and politics between my father and uncle Kim Duth. I have such clear memories of my uncle Kim Duth telling my father how he thought that communist was evil. He continued, "If the Khmer Rouge take over our country, they will kill all the people". My father did not agree with my uncle told me how he thought communism was good. "They treat people fairly, there are no classes in communism. People are equal in rights." He believed that socialism allowed all people to live comfortably and have their needs met regardless of the type or amount of work they did. He also believed that with socialism you could even enjoy many of life's luxuries. However, for human beings to reach this state of socialism their governments would first have to go through communism.

While King Sihanouk was on an official visit to France on March 18, 1970 General Lon Nol took over the leadership of Cambodia in a bloodless coup and established the Khmer Republic. With the help of the United States Lon Nol established himself as the President of the Khmer Republic. The reason of the coup was King Sihanouk had made a big mistake to allow the Viet Cong forces, North Vietnam to use our territory to fight the war with South Vietnam, supported by U.S president Nickson government. Cambodians were divided on this change. Most Cambodians from Phnom Penh and the provincial capitals supported the coup. In the large cities, provincial towns and throughout most of the rural areas,

Cambodians enjoyed peace. Many peasants and villagers from the countryside, however, did not support Lon Nol's coup. They were suffering from the ongoing civil war between government forces and the Khmer Rouge. They loved King Sihanouk who was the head of state.

During the mid-seventies the ideological struggle between capitalism and communism as well as efforts for world domination were being played out in Europe, Africa, Latin America and Asia. Consequently, this war reached our motherland, Cambodia where super-powers fought wars by plenipotentiary and viceroy. The former Soviet Union, USSR-backed Viet Cong forces of North Vietnamese supported Cambodia's Khmer Rouge in their fight to overthrow the US-backed government of Lon Nol. The Viet Cong intention is take over South Vietnam and to colony in Indo-China, Lao and Cambodia.

Among the factors contributing to Lon Nol's coup d'etat was King Sihanouk secret support with food and weapons for both the Khmer Rouge (KR) and the Viet Cong. The Viet Cong of North Vietnam supported and trained the Khmer Rouge resistant against the Lon Nol Government, back by the U.S government. King Sihanouk continued his support after the coup by allowing Viet Cong troops to remain in Cambodia to wage war against Lon Nol's government as well as against the government of South Vietnamese president Nguyen Van Thieu. The United States was providing support to both Lon Nol and Nguyen Van Thieu's governments.

Another factor contributing to the coup was how King Sihanouk violated the provisions of the Cambodian constitution prohibiting foreign troops to use Cambodia for military operations. With Sihanouk's knowledge, the Viet Cong troops in Cambodia tyrannized and killed many Cambodian peasants, farmers and villagers living in the war zone. These same Viet Cong troops used their strategic position to launch military operation against US forces fighting in South Vietnam. In turn, the U.S. bombed Viet Cong forces in Cambodia.

Some of King Sihanouk cabinet were also left and joined the Khmer Rouge, like Mr. Kiev Samphan who later became, an Evil Deputy Prime Minister in charge of Economic and Foreign Affairs and the main brain to the Democratic Kampuchea, Khmer Rouge Regime.

After the coup, King Sihanouk did not return to Cambodia but instead traveled to Russia and China to seek support. Finally, through his strong relationship with prime minister Zhou En Lai, Sihanouk was offered a villa in China. The Chinese government paid all of Sihanouk's living expenses. At that time, the friendship between Vietnam and China seem to be strong. With the help of the Chinese government and the Viet Cong, King Sihanouk was installed as the head of the Khmer Rouge Communist Movement, residing in China. King Sihanouk appealed on the radio to peasants, farmers and villagers to join Khmer Rouge troops to fight against Lon Nol's government. Hungry peasants, farmers and villagers migrated to the cities fleeing the Khmer Rouge (KR), the Viet Cong known as North Vietnam government and American bombing. There was thousand of Khmer Isarak (Khmer communist) who was trained by Hanoi government returned to fight the war against Lon Nol government.

King Sihanouk also appealed on both radio and television that "to join Khmer Rouge Communist Movement, is to fight for him, 'Eu' to resume back in power". So that he can help all peasants, farmers and villagers, known in Khmer as "Kon Chau".

The Khmer Rouge movement started recruiting peasants, farmers and villagers to join their communist army. They built up their armies day by day to fight against Lon Nol's government. With strong support from the large Viet Cong presence twenty five percent of rural areas were liberated and controlled by KR. They were building up their stronghold and occupied parts of western, northeast, northwest and southwest rural Cambodia. Peasant farmers and villagers who were not able to escape were forced to join the Khmer Rouge in order to survive. The Khmer Rouge controlled some of eastern and western rural areas. On a daily basis the Khmer Rouge would attack the provinces. There were many Khmer Rouge (KR) secret service agents who worked for Khmer Republic throughout Cambodia's cities, provinces, districts, communes and villages.

In 1973 Khmer Rouge forces with the collaboration of Vietcong forces of North Vietnam bombed and destroyed the Cambodian-Japanese friendship bridge at Chroy Chongvar in Phnom Penh. This same year the KR gathered their forces and with the help of the Viet Cong launched a massive military attack to take over the capital Phnom Penh. Their campaign, however, was thwarted by the strong U.S. air forces assisting Lon Nol. In addition to their military operations, the KR tried to win the hearts and souls of the Khmer people who live in countryside.

It reminded me about my cousins Ang and Sung who used to tell me story about how evil communism and North Vietnam (Vietcong) was and also uncle Kim Duth who used to have a discussion with my father about our country, Cambodia and the conflict with the North and South Vietnam could effects Cambodia in both economically, politically and militarily, communism and capitalism.

He told my father how evil, barbarous and cruel communism was. He continued to tell us about the North Vietnam invasion to Cambodia. King Sihanouk of Cambodia who was the Head of State during that time have to let the North Vietnam Forces to used our territory to exchange for peace and stability in the country. The first was the promised that the Vietcong forces will not invade Cambodia and second it's just used to escape from the U.S and South Vietnam Forces when there was a major fighting and air bombing.

I also heard and learned from old people saying that when north Vietnam take over south Vietnam, there was a promise and agreement by President Ho Chi Minh of North Vietnam with King Sihanouk of Cambodia that he will return part of Cambodian territory known as Kampuchea Krom that was cut by the French Government during their colony in IndoChina to Vietnam back to Cambodia Government.

Cambodia was a small country with small population. Therefore, we cannot stand with our big neighboring country like Vietnam unless we had modern and advance military technology.

In communist and socialist regime, the ruler said something and their action was completely different. They said this and what they did was opposite. Most communist leaders are dictator, evil and leader of killer. They are abuse power. One man controlled everything in the whole country. They are in the power for the rest of their life. There was no democracy in communism. This idea was always in my mind.

From China and North Vietnam they were able to broadcast to Cambodia their propaganda on revolutionary plans and activities as well as on the successes of their military operations which shown King Sihanouk visited liberation zones accompanied by his royal loyalist, Kiev Samphan, Hu Nim and Hou Youn. These two men, Hu Nim and Hou Youn, later were killed by his comrade in armed. He made a trip from China to North Vietnam then to Cambodia to visit liberation zones. This trip was to encourage KR forces and to show their victory that KR had control some part of the country. Their messages about the revolution were filled with lies claiming the benefits of their revolution for Cambodia and its people. But in fact the KR did many bad things. They killed people. They burned schools, hospitals, roads, and bridges. They were evil. Peasants, villagers and farmers with little education were easily brainwashed by them.

My father's friend, who was the head of an orphanage, learned that he was to be among the American diplomats, foreign officials and some large Cambodians to be evacuated by US Marine transport helicopters. He had also arranged for my brother Reagan and me to leave with him but he would not be able to take my youngest sister, Margaret, who was too young. My parents first agreed with the plan to let us leave Cambodia with his friend.

Ten days before Lon Nol's US-backed government collapsed, Reagan and I made our way to the building, US embassy near the

Independence Monument and riverside for the evacuation. US Marine helicopters came to Phnom Penh for "Operation Eagle Pull" landing near Building, along bassak river. This was the name the military gave to the evacuation. The helicopters landed on top of the US Embassy and on the park where evacuees were gathering. We would be airlifted out of Cambodia to a US Navy ship in the Gulf of Thailand.

The fleet of helicopters began airlifting people under the watch of armed US Marines. As Reagan and I made our way to the helicopter my father's friend told us that we could not board the helicopter. My parents called him not go let me and my brother go to America. They had changed their minds and didn't want us to go to America. We were their only sons. My parents told his friend that they loved us and couldn't imagine living without us. Reagan and I had to return home. We were very upset with our parents for not allowing us to leave Cambodia with my father's friend. During the US evacuation from Cambodia many Cambodian orphans were taken to America. Although we didn't escape from the Khmer Rouge our family was happy to know that my uncle Kim Duth did. After his graduation from Royal Phnom Penh University he went to Paris to do post graduate studies just before the Khmer Rouge take-over.

On April 10, 1975, one week before the fall of the Khmer Republic, my father's friends came to our home to say that the Khmer Rouge (KR) would probably take over the country within five days. He told my father to prepare the family for an immediate escape. Unfortunately my father did not believe him. My family was not the only one to doubt the take-over. In fact very few city-dwelling Cambodians thought that the Khmer Rouge would kill their own people. We all thought that since we all had the "same blood" the Khmer Rouge would treat people fairly and respect their rights. So many of us believed the Khmer Rouge were going to establish a classless society. The prevailing thought was that communism was good. Unfortunately, these were all misconceptions.

Before the fall, the Khmer Rouge attacked and bombed all areas near Pochentong International Airport and all areas near Phnom Penh, the capital of the Cambodia. The KR Eastern and Southwestern Divisions took over Neak Loeang. Then they moved on to Kandal province. The KR Western Division took over Kampong Speu. The goal was for all KR Divisions to move to Phnom Penh. Bombs, artillery shells and fires surrounded Phnom Penh day and night. The Khmer Republic army took a strong stand to defend the city but foods and supplies were cut off by road. The only food and supplies were delivered by airs and parachutes.

On the morning on April 17, 1975 the Khmer Rouge soldiers marched unopposed down the boulevards of a burning Phnom Penh. They had come to take over the city and to declare that this was Day Zero for the new Cambodia now to be called Democratic Kampuchea (DK). The soldiers were dressed in black military uniforms and hats. Around their necks was the Cambodia traditional scarf known as the "Kroma" and on their feet were simple sandals made of tire rubber. Some soldiers arrived on the backs of military trucks. Others were on motorcycles, while others rolled down the city streets in armored personnel carriers. They all carried AK47 rifles. At first, some Phnom Penh residents welcomed them with cheers of "Chey yoo pade vat", "Long live the revolution".

On that day, my immediate and extended family gathered in my uncle Song's villa, now it's near German Embassy. Crowded in there were my uncle Sokhak, my uncle Song and his family, my aunt Sa and her family, my aunt Sin and my aunt Sang and her family. Many villas, including my uncle's, had a white flag hanging out front, an indication to the Khmer Rouge (KR) that the occupants, including us, had surrendered. The flags were a message to the KR to not set the villa on fire. The brief moments of peace and happiness had now turned to fear, confusion and chaos. The army went from house to house in search of high-ranking officials from the Lon Nol government. The KR soldiers started the evacuation of people from Phnom Penh. All the people from the city, including my family, were forced to flee their homes. The Khmer Rouge soldiers shot and killed our uncle Song's next door neighbors who refused to leave their home. The whole family was killed including two toddlers. That day senseless violence and killings took place throughout the city.

On that day, city stores were robbed and loading by KR. They will kill those owners who refused to give out their valuable properties to the Khmer Rouge soldiers.

Almost five years old, I was so scared of the KR soldiers in their black uniforms. Most of them looked very cruel to me. They reminded me of an evils I would see in the movies who eat people alive. My Sister, Margaret and I was crying and crying. Mom and Dad told me not to cry. They told me that my crying could get my family and relatives in a lot of trouble. Then, I stopped crying. We were told that Angkar "Padevat"(the "Revolutionary Organization") had to clear the city. "The United States was going to bomb the city," they told us. Then went on to say that we would leave for only three days and then were expected to return. This was what Angkar told us.

My aunts, uncles and my family started packing just enough clothing and food for three days. Each of my relatives had their own car. My family convoy headed out of the city towards Neak Loeung. The streets were full of chaos and panic. People who did not have car used some sort of trolley to transport their belongings. Some people used a "Remork", a motorcycle with a small trailer hitched behind it, to transport their belongings. Other people used "cyclos" the three-wheeled cycle rickshaw, to transport their belongings. Those who did not have any means of transportation held their stuff in bags and just walked. We saw the Khmer Rouge soldiers shoot and kill people. Old people and children were crying. We had to pass through many KR checkpoints. Fortunately and thank God the KR we met were nice. We learned that they were members of the troops that were loyal to Sihanouk. Khmer Rouge soldiers ordered everyone, "Go! Go! Go!" On our way to the countryside we saw many Khmer Rouge soldiers. All the roads were jammed with city residents.

We saw wounded people, people with amputated limbs and people who had lost their family. We saw so many horrible things that we had never seen before. My father told my family and relatives to keep silent. He told us all that if we were asked by KR soldiers about our occupations we should lie to them and say that we were cyclo drivers, lampata taxi drivers, waiters and waitresses in restaurant or simple food sellers. He told us to keep a low profile and hiding our background in order to survive. You could not tell anyone about your background and occupation.

When we passed by the next Khmer Rouge checkpoint which were jammed with all the evacuees, two Khmer Rouge soldiers approached my father and called him, "Comrade", "Comrade, Angkar need doctors, teachers, engineers, intellectuals and those who used to work for Lon Nol Government as soldier or any positions to help out the country in reconstruction and destroy the American imperialism and feuds. Angkar needs to know everyone's occupation. Do you do any of the work that I just mentioned, Comrade"? Dad replied, "No, I am lampata taxi driver. Then the same question was asked of my uncles and aunts. A KR cadre also approached the cars stopped in front of us. We recognized him as a cadre by the pistol he had on his waist. He said, "Comrade, Comrade, Angkar needs your help to cure our wounded soldiers".

The KR soldier noticed the man's light skin, an indication that he did not work out in Cambodia's hot sun. The man replied, "No comrade, I am not a doctor, I am an engineer. The KR cadre said, "Yes, yes you are the one that Angkar is looking for. You have to come with us and help Angkar to install industrial electricity." The man replied, "No comrade, I have a family, a wife, old grandparents and two children that I have to take good care of." The KR cadre replied, "Angkar will take good care of them. Don't worry." The man still refused to go with him. Finally he was bitten by the cadre, handcuff and tossed like an animal into a military truck and taken away. The man's wife ran and followed her husband. She stopped and grabbed the KR soldiers in an effort to get her husband back. She was bitten by the cadre and shot in her legs. The grandparents and the woman's children started crying for help.

My dad realized that the situation was getting worse and told us all to prepare to escape. Another KR soldier approached my father and said, "Comrade, Angkar needs all of these automobiles to use for national interest". My dad replied, "Sorry, Comrade we really need this car for transportation". Then we heard many shoots from around the corner. Khmer Rouge soldiers were shooting anyone who refused to give up their valuables. Fancy watches, gold necklaces, earrings, bracelets, motorcycles and automobiles all were to be given to Angkar. Some people in the crowd began to fight back and surrounded one KR soldier. They tried to grab his gun and were fighting to defend themselves. I looked on in horror as KR soldiers shot innocent citizens. Blood flowed and spilled all over the roads. In shock I screamed "Oh my God, oh my God". Frightened, I closed my eyes and started crying and stunned. Another KR soldier quickly opened fired in the air to threaten those people who were bold enough to fight. Then the soldier turned and ran back to his team.

All this confusion had fortunately worked to our advantage. My dad, uncles and cousins realized that this would be a good time to for us to flee from the chaos. Because the soldiers could not remember whom they had spoken to we were able to escape without being followed. The plan was for the men and women to split up. The men in my family would follow my dad and the women would follow my mom. My dad told my mom that a one of his friend's would meet us on the other side of the River in Neak Loeung. We had to leave most of our belongings in our cars and carried only the basics: clothing, a frying pan and some rice and dried fish. My mom, aunts and small cousins took the ferry to the other side of the River and arrived in Neak Loeung where we happily met up with my dad and uncles. During the course of that day in Neak Loeung we noticed heaps of ammunition that had been left behind by Lon Nol's soldiers. That evening the whole family spent the night together in Neak Loeung before we would continue our exile from Phnom Penh.

Our family brought a lot of money with us. So on our way to Smoung village, we tried to buy things and food to eat. We were told by sellers that "Angkar said: money was no use any more". Foods and all things were trade with gold, diamond like earing, necklace, citizen watch and with valuable.   From then, market businesses were disappeared forever.

After three weeks of walking carrying our food we finally arrived in the village of Smoung. This small village is located within the commune of Samlanh in the Angkor Chey District, Takeo province. This is about two miles from the Tramkak District on the borders of Takeo and Kampot provinces. This is where my father lived during his childhood. When he turned eighteen my father left his village to come to Phnom Penh to go to the University. My dad's older brother, Uncle Harn, still lived there and was a farmer. The Khmer Rouge considered my uncle Harn as a "neak moulthan" or one of "the base people". All those who lived in the KR liberated zones during the war were called "base people". On the other hand, the KR classified my family as well as my aunts, uncles and cousins from the city as "neak thmei" or "the new people". All the people from the cities, and provincial towns like ourselves, were classified as these "neak thmei" or "the new people"

Uncle Harn's family welcomed our entire family and relatives. We lived there for a few months. Initially we were allowed to move about with relative freedom. But during that time we eagerly awaited news from Angkar that our family could return to Phnom Penh. Dad's brother, Harn, told him that we should not think about returning to Phnom Penh. Angkar had started a campaign of registering people who worked for the Khmer Republic. Angkar told them that they could go back to Phnom Penh to work for Angkar as its eyes and ears, as the intellect that Angkar needed. But this story was a lie. If you registered, you would be forced to attend revolutionary reeducation training. Angkar had already started sending the new people, "neak thmei", to this revolutionary training. When they said, "Angkar needs you to attend revolutionary training" it meant that you would be taken off and killed. During our stay with my uncle Harn he told us many of Angkar's evil deeds.

According to dad and uncle Song said " the evacuation of city and provincial residents has been made by the Khmer Rouge

14

(KR) hardliner group rank as follow, Pol Pot, Head of Kampuchea Communist Party (KCP) and of the Democratic Kampuchea (DK), Ieng Sary, Foreign and International Affair Minister, Noun Chea, Head of Parliament, and Son Sen", Defense Minister. This idea of evacuation had been dispute with other KR loyalist, Sihanoukist who pro-Vietnamese: So Phim, Eastern Zone Secretary, Hu Nim, Hou Youn, [Chau Seng, and Phouk Chhay were the prominent Khmer leftist educated from France] , Chou Chet, DK Western Zone Secretary and other DK members.

Democratic Republic of Kampuchea (DRK) – Khmer Rouge (KR) 1975-1976
My Life in the Evil Khmer Rouge Regime

After the American government supported the fall of Khmer Republic, the communist took over Cambodia and established a government called " Democratic Republic of Kampuchea". This government was supported by Vietnam and China.

Democratic Republic of Kampuchea led by comrade Pol Pot who was party general secretary and head of the DRK. His government was formed by Nuon Chea, head of national assembly, Ieng Sary, Foreign and International cooperation minister, Son Sen, National Defense and Interior minister, Khiev Samphan, later was assigned to be president of democratic republic of Kampuchea and also in charge of finance and economic after the resignation of King Sihanouk and so on.

Pol Pot, inspired by Mao Zedong's Cultural Revolution of communist China, then attempted to build his own agrarian utopia in Cambodia, which he established the Democratic Republic of Kampuchea. He said that his society under his leadership has no classes. Every one was equal. But it was totally different. Comrade Pol Pot hardly appeared in the public. He disguised his identity. No one know that he was the head of the DRK.

This evil communist regime destroyed everything, which included businesses, school, hospital, market, Buddhist temple,

16

church, national infrastructures and killing millions of his owned people. Any foreign economic or medical assistance was rejected. Thus, Cambodia became sealed off from the outside world. This was the most evil regime in Cambodian history.

While we were in hiding my parents told me that I cried a lot and would say that I wanted to go back home to Phnom Penh. Life was so different and not what we were used to. My dad said, " I am looking for a way for us to go back home". He and the rest of the family secretly discussed how we could flee Cambodia and head off to another country, maybe Vietnam. We lived just on the border of Kampot and Takeo provinces, which shared a border with the Socialist Republic of Vietnam. My uncle Song urged us to go to Thailand. To get there we would have to travel west through Kampong Speu, passed Pursat and on towards Battambang. Then we would reach the Thai border. In general everyone liked my uncle's idea but after some discussions we realized that it was too dangerous to travel. We would have to pass many Khmer Rouge checkpoints. Also we didn't have any mean of transportation and walking could take us months. At the end we decided to escape to Vietnam.

Day by day we learned about the changes taking place in our country and the latest developments with Angkar, high communist organization. The Khmer Rouge had even placed restrictions on travel within Cambodia. We learned from some local 'base people' whose sons were serving in the Khmer Rouge army that all of Cambodian borders with Thailand, Lao and Vietnam had been closed within six days after the April [17]th, 1975 "Liberation Day". Angkar had troops deployed along Cambodia's borders with Thailand, Lao and Vietnam. The Vietnam border was an especially well guarded one. Angkar did not want people moving anywhere without permission.

There were newly established security controls throughout the country. People were not allowed to talk to each other. We were not allowed to travel or even walk to neighboring villages. Traveling now was prohibited unless you had a good reason and the approval from your local village *(Angkar phum)*, commune *(khum)*, district *(srok)* and provincial authorities *(khet)*. Anyone caught breaking these rules was considered as a traitor to the revolution. This action would be killed.

In order for us to survive my dad, uncles, cousins and aunts would go fishing every day with their nets. Our family also did a bit of farming, growing potatoes and sugar cane. We were fortunate to know some kind-hearted base villagers from Smoung who helped us out with gifts of fruit and rice.

With time we came to learn of the worsening situation in Cambodia. Angkar had cut off relationship with the outside world and plunged the country into complete isolation. They then turned their focus on the Khmer people and divided them into two distinct groups. In the first group were the 'base people' known as *neak molthan* from the countryside who used to help the Khmer Rouge during the revolutionary war. The second group known as the *neak thmei* or group April 17 *Dab pram pi mesa* 'new people' from the city. This was the group my family belonged to. In this new Cambodian society the 'base' people' were considered as the new higher classes. They were to be the eyes and ears of Angkar and were given permission to move about freely within where they lived. 'New people' like us were now considered as the lowest members and the enemy of this new society. Angkar encouraged the base people, higher classes to constantly spy on the 'new people' in any way possible.

By end of August 1975, four months after the KR take-over, basic freedoms were prohibited. Cambodians could no longer speak their minds. Furthermore, we were not permitted to walk or travel wherever we wanted. In addition, the Khmer Rouge closed all schools, universities and pagodas. They even closed hospitals. Money, markets, traders and banks were all abolished in Pol Pot's efforts to achieve a radical Maoist State. In this communist utopia there was no place for teachers or professors or for scholars or intellectuals. Pol Pot also had no need for engineers, doctors or civil servants nor did he and his followers have any need for the petty bourgeois. The bourgeois were among the first to be eliminated from society. Furthermore, Cambodians could no longer practice their religion. Throughout the country Buddhist monks and Christian priests were defrocked and forced to lead civilian lives. They would be sent for revolutionary training, which meant death for many of them. Some fortunate ones were able to escape. With these changes we could see that the country quickly was heading into a sad downward spiral.

By September 1975 Angkar had established collectivized cooperatives known as *sahakor*. The *sahakors* were where all the 'new people' went to eat. The Khmer Rouge did not allow 'new people' to keep food in their homes. We 'new people' were also not allowed to eat at home. However the members of the 'base people' groups were allowed to keep food at home and to take their meals at home.

The Khmer Rouge established local authorities known as *prothean* to help them govern at the village, commune and district levels. They maintained a militia drawn from the men and women of rural backgrounds and further complemented their control mechanism with both child and adult militia messengers known as *kong chlob*. They also recruited soldiers for each of the five DK military regions in the country.

All families and individuals were ordered to give up all of their personal possessions. Watches and jewelry were taken away. Even simple belongings such as pots, pans and dishes as well as our own food was taken from us. All these things now belonged to *Angkar Leou*, the high communist organization. Angkar told every one " those who hide things and do not give up all their personal belonging to Angkar will be considered as a traitor of Angkar Leou. Anyone caught hiding personal belongings from Angkar risked being killed.

Angkar ordered each family to work in the rice fields of their respective village, commune and district. We were forced to grow three rice harvests a year. We also had to dig dams and canals for irrigation. Angkar began recruiting and drafting children into a children's concentration camp known as *kong koma*. Adults were herded into mobile concentration camps known as *kong yuvachun* and *kong chalat*.

19

The Khmer Rouge regularly moved their main labor forces of adult and youth mobile concentration camps from place to place. As soon as a project was finished the mobile teams would receive orders from Angkar to move their camp on to the next project. My uncle Sokhak, aunt Sang, aunt Sin as well as my cousins Ang and Sung were forced to participate in the *kong chalat* mobile concentration camps. Angkar forced my uncle Song and his family to move to another village. The same went for my aunt Sang and her family. They were not allowed to live within their own family and village. Angkar separated families, husbands and wives, sons and daughters and relatives.

As the situation in the country worsened my family realized that our relationship with my uncle Harn could get us all in trouble. In fact, if other "base people" told Angkar that he had relatives from Phnom Penh we would all be killed. My dad thought it was best for us not to speak to him anymore and pretend that we didn't know him. We only spoke to him in secret and made certain that no one saw us. Angkar place a further strain on our personal lives by forbidding Cambodian children to use the usual forms of *"Pa"* and *"Mak"* for "dad" and "mom" and ordered us all to use the new revolutionary terms *"Puk"* and *"Me"*. If Angkar heard anyone using the old forms of address the whole family could be purged.

My immediate family was able to remain together until early January 1976. One evening we were secretly enjoying a family dinner in our cottage, something that Angkar definitely forbid. While dining I noticed a horse-drawn cart stop in front of our cottage. On the cart were three Khmer Rouge soldiers with AK-47 rifles. They were dressed in the typical black uniforms and rubber sandals with the traditional Cambodian scarves around their necks. We panicked and quickly hid our food and pots. Our first thought was that they found out that we had prepared our own food and we were enjoying dinner in our cottage. We soon learned why they came.

One soldier asked for my father. He pointed his finger at my dad and said, "Are you comrade Phorn? " My dad replied, "Yes, that is me, comrade". The soldier then said, "I have orders from Angkar to take you for revolutionary re-education training". He continued,

"Comrade, you will not need to take anything with you". My father then turned to say goodbye and told my mom to take good care of us. The KR soldiers then told my father, "Comrade, you need not worry about them, Angkar will take good care of them".

He then added, "Comrade, *you* need to worry because you will be sent to the front line, *samora phum muk*. We understood the sad and cruel meaning behind his comment - the village we lived in was called *samora phum krauy* or Back Line Village. My father remained silent and walked out of our cottage with the soldiers. They tied him up, put him on the cart and then drove away. We all stood there, watching him being led away. We wanted to run to help him but there was nothing we could do to help him. We were just small children. If we risked doing anything we would all have been in trouble. We just stood there and watched as the cart disappeared into horizon. That evening my mom told us that we lost our dad. They would probably kill him. She continued, "Dad is a smart man and he might be able to escape". We all felt so sad about the loss of my father and worried about our future.

The Khmer Rouge did not distribute food rations evenly but instead distributed them based on your class. 'Base people' were given more food than 'new people'. They also were permitted to cook and eat at home. 'New people' like us had to go to our local cooperative "*sahakor*" to eat where Angkar gave us our daily rations.

Within a short amount of time it seemed that our situation worsened day by day. By this time Angkar had learned all about our backgrounds. They pressured and warned all 'base people' to cut off any ties with the 'new people'. They forced these people to spy on us new people and find out about everyone's family background and occupations from the previous Lon Nol regime. The 'base people' were considered to be the trusted eyes and ears of Angkar.

Despite Angkar's restrictions on contact between the 'new people' and the other classes of people our uncle Harn secretly helped us in many ways. He gave us sugar cane and palm juice and hides chicken and duck eggs in the forest so that our family had enough food to eat.

Four weeks after the Khmer Rouge soldiers had taken my dad away my brother Reagan was assigned to force to leave us and join a *kong komar,* children's mobile team concentration camp. The Khmer Rouge was tearing apart not only our family one by one but the whole families in the country. My mother realized what was happening and told us that we would have to move to Phum Prey Toting, Prey Toting village. At this point our family had been reduced to my mom, my sister Margaret and me. Angkar questioned us before allowing us to settle there. Margaret and I lived there for about two months and then finally moved to Nang Sahet village. My mom, Margaret and I lived together until early 1976 when my mother was assigned to join women's mobile team concentration camp. At only six years old my family had been reduced to my sister and me. Fortunately one day Margaret and I met our aunt Sar who was also living in the same village. We asked if we could stay with her and she said it would be ok. She was lucky to be granted permission to stay in that village because she had given birth to Veasna, a baby boy. Veasna means destiny in Khmer. My sister and I thought that her son brought her good luck.

By December 1976, at six and a half years old, I was forced to join the children's village team. I was the youngest member of the team and actually considered too young to be a part of it. The chief of children's local team told me that when I came to work I would have to go to the *sahakor* to report to *mit bong,* chief of the children's team before going out to work. My workday ran from 6:30 to 11:30 in the morning, and from 1:00 to 5:00 in the afternoon. My job was to take care of cows, oxen and buffalos and collect their dung. I also had to collect leaves from the Siam Weed the tropical shrub known in Khmer as *doeum kantreang khet.* The leaves of this plant were used as fertilizer.

Because I was so small I had a lot of trouble controlling these animals. One day I was assigned to take care of two male water buffalos known in Khmer as *krobei lengkor.* One was good-natured and the other one was so nasty to me. The nasty one had a strong muscular neck. When I took them to the fields I would let them eat grass and then take them for some water in a nearby small dam. One day near the end of my morning shift I was waiting for the sound of the *chuong* or gong used to alert the workers that it was time to eat at the *sahakor*. On my way there, the nasty buffalo broke free of his rope and wandered off to another village. I quickly jumped on the back of my good buffalo and charged off fetch him but couldn't. I was upset and knew that I had to report what happened to the chief of the local children's team *mit bong*, at the *sahakor.*

"Oh, boy", *mit bong* said. "You committed a minor infraction. "Angkar will not give you any food this morning because you failed to carry out the task Angkar gave you." This was a formal warning, a *korsang*. She added, "You will need to see Angkar". When she left I began to cry because I was sad and hungry. I was seated near the *sahakor* when a young girl came up to me. Her name was Roeun. She was nine years old and was the daughter of the village chief. She saw tears rolling down my cheeks and asked me, "Why are you crying?" I held back my sobs knowing well that Angkar considered sobbing a crime. I answered, "One of my buffalos ran off to another village and Angkar is punishing me by not allowing me to eat. I am starving". She then told me to wait until everyone had left and she would then bring me some food. She did not want anyone seeing her give me food. I felt so happy.

That afternoon, I had to go with the *mit bong* to get my buffalo back from the nearby village called, Sdok. When we arrived I was happy to see my buffalo. I walked over to it and said, "This is my buffalo, Mit Bong". She spoke to the local village chief and my buffalo was released. That evening, Angkar only allowed me to have small dinner at *sahakor,* reducing my portion as punishment. I was given a very small portion of *bor bor,* Cambodian rice porridge, and the soup made from *trakuon,* a Khmer plant known in English as water morning glory.

Most children in my village were either from the 'base people, higher class except me and two other children who were from the 'new people' from the city. The 'base children had been trained to hate the 'new people'. They called us, imperialists, *ar puk chak kropoot* because we were from the capital. When people address someone with the prefix *ar* in Khmer it is considered to be an insult. Sometimes they would kick us and slap us in the face. They regularly threw small stones and dirt at us. *Mit bong* would not scold them or say anything to them about their unacceptable behavior. The children would say, "You can not do anything because my parents are *kammar pibaal* or high ranking officials in DK regime. All 'new people' including children were considered to be the lowest class in Democratic Kampuchea society. The Khmer Rouge treated us badly. They did not give us enough food and as a result we all became very thin and lacked energy. After a hard day's work the 'new people' had to wait for the sound of the *chuong* summoning us to our lunch and dinner at the collective cooperative community, *sahakor*.

In early 1977 the Khmer Rouge started implementing their social revolutionary changes that included a campaign of mass massacre and killing throughout the country. They were in the midst of changing everything; even the way people got married. Large marriage ceremonies would be held for as many as 10 to 50 couples at a time. Initially Angkar would collect men and women from different mobile teams and concentration camps. Then they would screen the selected and do background checks to see if anyone have been involved with the Lon Nol regime. Then the Khmer Rouge would force them to marry. We Cambodians had to follow their instructions if we wanted to survive. They would be forced to exchange simple vows and then they would be considered as married. If anyone disagreed Angkar would accuse him or her of being a traitor to the revolutionary and then they would be killed.

King Sihanouk gave the name *Khmer Krahom* or Red Cambodians or Khmer Rouge to the Cambodian communists. The Khmer Rouge was divided into two groups. One group consisted of the pro-Pol Pot hard-liners who were supported by China. The other group was made up of a small group of pro-Sihanouk supporters known as the *Khmer Rumdos, remained from Khmer Isarak (Khmer communist).* Communist of Vietnam supported them. Although this group controlled the eastern and southeastern provinces of Prey Veng, Svay Rieng, Kandal, Takeo and Kampot their support proved powerless against strongmen like Pol Pot, Ieng Sary, Noun Chea, Son Sen, Keo

Puk and Ta Mouk who has strong mechanism power and controlled the rest of the country.

At the end of January 1977 Angkar sent me back to Prey Toting to live while my sister remained with my aunt in Nang Sahet. From that point my sister Margaret and I only saw each other on rare occasions. By this time the Khmer Rouge had completely separated my immediate family as well as Cambodian in the country.

After King Sihanouk returned from China, he was assigned by Pol Pot to be the president of Democratic Republic of Kampuchea (DRK) with the recommendation from Chinese government. Pol Pot did not like this idea.

But to have their good relationship with the People's Republic of China, Pol Pot has to assign King Sihanouk to be the president. During the Khmer Rouge regime, Pol Pot, Ieng Sary and Noun Chea and his group controlled all the power. The powerless president of Democratic Republic of Kampuchea, King Sihanouk. By seeing the Khmer Rouge killed intellectual people by this bloodshed regime, closed down hospitals, churches, Buddhist temples, Money, markets, traders and banks were all abolished. This DRK cut off from the outside world, by seeing this, later the King requested his resignation. And later he became the Khmer Rouge prisoner in his own Royal Palace.

Phum = village, hamlet
Phumipheak = zone/region (DK usage)
Srok = district
Trokuon = water morning glory, a nutritious Khmer plant
Wat   = Buddhist monastery
Krom = work team
Khum = commune, subdistrict
Kong Chalat = DK mobile work brigade, mostly composed of young workers
Prahoc = Khmer preserved fish paste
Krom = Lowest unit of social control in Cambodia

Democratic Republic of Kampuchea (DRK) – Khmer Rouge (KR) 1977
My Life in the Evil Khmer Rouge Regime

In early January 1977 I was able to escape to Prey Toting village. When I arrived there I was forced to join the children mobile team. Angkar had just received an order that all children were allowed to attend school. Because of what they thought was we were the new seeds for Angkar and Cambodia. Angkar claimed it had no connection with the previous imperialist regime. All of the children including myself were so happy to go to school because we were able to have a break from physical labor. We attended school for one and a half hours a day three times a week. We were taught basic Khmer consonant and vowel. Under the DK regime there was no standard school for children. Our classrooms consisted of a simple blackboard placed under the shade of a big tree with a blackboard. Our teachers were uneducated DK cadres. Within two or three months, I did not remember, by March 1977, Angkar changed its policy and banned this short-lived education campaign.

In April 1977 Angkar ordered everyone to work day and night for up to 16 hours a day. We were given very little food each day, small portion of rice porridge and water lily soup. Many people started died of starving and dead bodies could be seen lying along the edge of roads with short forest grow along like pile of garbage. As part of children team, I worked up to 14 hours per day. By this time my job was becoming more and more difficult. The children's team had to assist the Adult, Youth and Mobile Teams digging dams and canals, growing rice, corn, bean and potatoes. Nineteen seventy-seven, 1977 proved to be one of the most difficult years for all the 'new people'.

In 1977, although most us Cambodians were starving, the Khmer Rouge decided to export 95% of the country's crops to China. These crops included rice, corn, beans, cotton, sugar palm and sugar cane, basic items of the Khmer diet. The Khmer Rouge also exported 95% of the country's domestic and wild livestock as well as rubber. In exchange the People's Republic of China provided Cambodia with weapons and ammunition. China also sent thousands of military advisors to assist the DK regime. The remaining 5% of food produced in Cambodia first went to the top leaders of Angkar and whatever was left over went to the people.

We were forced to work hard day and night, often to the point of collapse. During this time many Cambodians died of hunger. I, as well as many Cambodians, had no energy and often fell sick. Our food portions were very small and the general quality of the food was very poor. If we talked about food sanitation is zero. During this time there were no hospitals or doctor's offices. There also weren't any professionally trained doctors or medical practitioners. The Khmer Rouge had them all killed off. What we had instead were basic health centers staffed with uneducated medical workers. The Khmer Rouge killed off all doctors and trained medical professionals. We did not have any medicines and the Khmer Rouge was forced to use coconut juice as an IV solution.

There were many unimaginable things we ate like frogs, toads, mice, and ants as well as a whole variety of lizards. We ate anything we could in order to survive. I got very sick a few times because I ate poisonous lizards. The local cures for these poisonous animals were sugar palm and the juice of honeybees. Lots of people died as a result of eating "kengkuk", the same poisonous toads and lizard I ate.

When I got sick I was unable to work and asked the chief of the children's mobile team if I could stay at home and rest at home like the 'base people' did when they were sick. Instead, the chief ordered that I go to work. She told me that I was not really sick but instead was suffering from emotional problems because I missed my family. She barked "You have to go to work tomorrow!". She continued, "If you do not go to work tomorrow, Angkar would charge you with a serious infraction or "kosang". Even as a child, I knew that Angkar killed many people based on mere accusations. They would say "Chom Nheur Sate Arom". What it means was emotional problem, not really sick.

The next morning I got up feeling tired and lacking in strength and tried to walk to work. On my way to work I felt very dizzy and couldn't see clearly. Everything became dark around me. Then I collapsed and felled onto the path of rice field called "Pleu Sre".

Fortunately "Loon", the chief of Prey Toting village found me. He was one of the Khmer Rouge's killers. At first he thought I was dead but when he realized I was not he helped me regain consciousness. It was unbelievable that a killer like "Loon" could have any sympathy and want to help me. This kind of help must come from our Almighty God, Jesus Christ who makes Loon's heart to willing to spare my life.

He ordered Grandma Roeun who was a base people to take care of me since I did not have any family in this village. He told her that I should stay with her until I regained my health. Loon reported my sickness to "Mit Bong", Chief of Children Mobile Concentration Team that same day.

Eight hours later I woke up crying with tears running down my cheeks. My whole body was in pain and I could fee that some of my organs were swollen. Under the DK many people suffered from this swelling called "Chom Nheu Hoeum" in Khmer caused by lacked of food ration and vitamins. I felt so exhausted and tired without sufficient food to give strength to my body. I didn't even have the strength to walk. I asked Grandma Roeun if she had any food for me. She replied "No". I said to myself, "Oh God, how will I get any food if I can't walk to the local cooperatives, *sahakor*". She insisted that I eat at the *sahakor* and not at her house. The dining hour had passed and even if the *sahakor* had remained open I wouldn't have been able to walk there. She was very nasty and mean to me. But this type of behavior was not restricted to Grandma Roeun but was prevalent among most of 'base people' who were very nasty and mean to us 'new' people.

Before my mother was taken to the mobile concentration camp she told us that if we need any food we should ask our village chief for permission to go see our mother. I now remembered those words. She told us she would secretly trade with the 'base people' to get some food and sugar for us. My sister and I had to keep this secret, she told us, since Angkar considered such trading as a serious infraction or "kosang". In fact, if Angkar found out that she was doing this secret trading it would be a death sentence for the whole family.

Then an idea came to me. I told Grandma Roeun who was a base people that if she gave me some food and palm sugar to eat I would give her some gold, a gold earring or a watch that I found a long time ago. I told her that I hid them in the forest near Sdok, my old village. In fact, I did not have any of these items. I just invented the story and fortunately she believed it. "I want the gold earring", she told me. She warned me that if I did not give her the gold earring she would tell Angkar to kill me. I told her I would definitely give it to her and then asked her to help me obtain permission to stay in the village till I regained my health.

Thank God she believed me and I was able to rest. During my stay with Grandma Roeun I was able to eat two meals a day of good food such as fish, chicken, fruits and sugar palm and coconut juice. "Mit Bong" regularly checked with Grandma Roeun regularly to see if I had recovered. As soon as I did Grandma Roeun was to send me back to "Mit Bong" so that I could be put back to work to help achieve Angkar's revolutionary tasks.

Grandma Roeun told Mit Bong, "I definitely want to release him to you Comrade, but he is still seriously ill and sometimes he loses his consciousness". "Actually" she continued, "I don't want him in my house but Comrade "Loon" asked me to take him in until he was well enough to send back to the children's concentration camp. After "Mit Bong" asked about my condition she left.

Three weeks later I started to feel a bit better. The general swelling I experienced had subsided. But now, after my swollen had broken out. I had skin problem. The broken have swollen caused wounded and scars on my skin, organ and body. I was so happy to have a chance to stay in the village that I can have enough food to eat.

I asked Grandma Roeun about the women mobile concentration camp that Cambodian women were forced to join. She told me that it was located in Sdok and Doeum Por tree village. This camp gathered women and men from villages, districts and provinces such as Smoung, Nang Sahet, Prey Toting, Ong Chot and so on.

Six weeks later, with Grandma Roeun's permission I first went to visit my sister at a different village. I asked her if she wanted to go to see Mom with me and we both made a trip to Sdok village. On our way to Sdok village we saw lots of rotting dead bodies being eaten by birds and flies. The smell was horrendous. These people died either at the hands of Angkar or as a result of sickness. Somehow because we were so starving we were not afraid of the dead bodies and did not even think of ghosts. My sister and I just marched on toward "sahakor" where we found our mother. Mom panicked when she saw us. Our visit could be a serious crime or "Kosang" for her. Our visit could have resulted in her being taken away for revolutionary re-education. We all knew that if Angkar sent someone to revolutionary re-education they disappeared forever as this re-education meant death.

Right away we assured Mom that we had permission. This made her feel better. But then the chief of mom's mobile concentration camp approached us and mom once again became nervous. Mit bong asked mom, "Who are these two children?" Mom replied with a trembling voice, "Mit bong, they are mine". "They came with the permission of Angkar." Mit bong asked, "Where is their permission letter?" She checked it and then gave it back to me. She ordered me to keep it in case we needed to cross the borders of any other village. If I did not have it then I would be captured and punished by Angkar.

She continued to blame our mother by saying "Angkar does not let children visit their own parents. All children belong to Angkar and are no longer your own. Next time do not let them visit you. Angkar will take care of them. Their visit makes you suffer from emotional sickness". This was known in Khmer as "Chom Ngeur Sate Arom". After scolding Mom, Mit Bong left. Mom was happy that Mit Bong did not accuse her of committing a serious crime.

At this brief family gathering we all noticed how dirty and skinny we looked. My mother asked my sister and I how we were doing. I told her about my illness and about Grandma Roeun. I explained how when I was sick I promised to give Grandma Roeun a gold earring in exchange for food. When she heard the story my mother became so sad. We all felt like crying but mom stopped us. If Angkar found out that we were crying they might kill us.

That evening my mother took her food ration from *sahakor* and we all shared it. My sister and I were not allowed to have any food since the chief at the *sahakor* considered us to be outsiders. After dinner mom gave me her gold earring. She took us to a village where she secretly traded in her gold with 'base people" for sugar palm, potatoes and dry rice which we shared amongst ourselves.

After we came back from the village where we got the food my mother said that she had to go back to her camp and that we couldn't stay with her. Angkar would not allow children to stay in this camp so my sister and I had to make our trip back that night. We walked through forest in the dark. On a few occasions when the clouds cleared we were fortunate enough to have the light of the full moon. As small children we felt very frightened walking alone through the forest at night. We were very lucky not to meet any KR

militia messengers who would have taken our food. We reached
Nang Sahet village where my sister live around 3:00 AM. I told her
to hide the food so that if she did not get enough food at the *sahakor*
she would have something to eat. After seeing her off I headed to
Prey Toting village where I lived.

Fortunately we arrived safely without meeting any militiamen
or militia messengers "Kong Chlop". We could have gotten into
serious trouble for having food with us. The simple act of having
this food, which we badly needed, was considered a crime according
to the Khmer Rouge authorities.

The next morning, when Grandma Roeun asked me about the
gold earring, I told her that I would give it to her. But I had a
feeling that it might be best to wait a few days. I thought that if I
gave it to her right away she might send me right back to children
mobile team. However, over the next few days, I noticed she once
again started to be means to me. I then decided to give her only one
earring instead of the pair. That way I could be on the safe side. She
was so happy to see such a beautiful gold earring. I told her I heard
the earring was considered valuable during the previous regime of
the Khmer Republic.

Grandma Roeun asked me to help her get some *sdao*, a particular
bitter-tasting tree leaf. She told me she wanted to eat it with *prahoc*,
Cambodian preserved fish paste. She went with me to the forest
near our village. I claimed up the *sdao* tree and cut a lot of leaves for
her. She shouted to me, "Collacot, go to the edge and cut the fresher
and younger leaves". As I got closer to the end of the branch I lost
my balance. I fell and hit my head on the edge of a creek. With the
sharp blow to my head I passed out. Grandma Roeun, thinking that
I was dead, left me behind and just went back to the village.

A passer-by found me lying down on the creek and helped me
out. He tried to resuscitate me by pressing the palms of his hands on
my chest. My head and arms were bloody. My whole body was full
of pain again. Although I was able to breathe I could not see clearly.
The passer-by asked me where I lived. I told him that I did not

have a home but was temporarily staying with Grandma Roeun. He carried me to Grandma Roeun's house. When we arrived Grandma Roeun was surprised and shocked to see that I was still alive. Oh, my God, this was again another help from unidentified people; this must be from God again. Who can walk a cross villages during the Khmer Rouge, you were either arrested or killed.

She yelled at me saying, "You survived just to be a burden to Angkar. It is no loss if Angkar destroys you." She continued. "All you 'new people' are trouble makers", *apok dob pram pi mesa.* I just kept quiet. Although she did not like me she was under the orders of Comrade "Loon" to house and look after me.

One day Mit Bong and comrade "Loon" came to see me at Grandma Roeun 's house. They were wondering why it was taking me so long to get well again. They questioned Grandma Roeun about my health. Grandma Roeun told them that I was seriously ill and that she did not have any medicines to give me. They asked her to see me. My head and arms were covered with traditional rural bandages. I could hardly open my mouth to talk to them because of the pain and swelling. They asked her what happened to me. She made up a story and told them that I climbed up a coconut tree to get something to eat and fell down.

They both got very angry with me and blamed me for stealing Angkar's coconuts and property. While Comrade Loon seemed to have sympathy for me Mit Bong did not. She angrily said, "He lived just to be a heavy burden to Angkar." She continued, "If Angkar destroys him it will not be any loss". After that they both left.

I was allowed to stay with Grandma Roeun until the end August of 1977. Day by day I started to feel myself slowly recovering from my sickness. One day, as I was still recovering, Mit Bong told me that I would have to go back to the children's mobile team located near our village. She said, "Angkar will send you to a different children mobile team located in Doeum Por village near Ant Mountain, *Phnom Sro Moch.* She continued, "Angkar did you a big favor by not

33

accusing you of a serious crime or *kosang*. Instead, you will be sent to the front line to help Angkar. You must be thankful to Angkar.

From then on, I started thinking of ways to escape to another village. Each day as my children mobile team walked across different villages, I would ask people about their village and their *sahakor* or cooperative community.

I often dreamt of and longed for the old days, my home and the Petit Lycee Bayon where I went to school in Phnom Penh. I would remember how much fun we would have during our weekly family gatherings and picnics. I remembered the times when my dad would drive me around to see new and different places. I realized how lucky I was then, living with my family in Phnom Penh at a time when the country was at peace. But sometimes I would suffer from nightmares in which Angkar sent me off for punishment. When I had these nightmares I would wake up and cry quietly through most of the night. I felt frightened of Angkar, not knowing what would happen to me, even imagining the worst, that I would be killed. My only thoughts were to escape to some other village where I could have enough food to eat and to stay with the better treated children from the countryside, *koon neak moulthan*.

During the Khmer Rouge period I was punished for escaping from the villages. I refused to join the children's mobile team. The chief of the children's mobile team with the assistance from the local militia chased me into the deep forest and captured me. She tyrannized, hit, stabbed me with a stick, and tried to force me to kill myself. I had to dig a hole, which was to be my grave while the guard of the local militia held an AK-47 rifle on me. When I finished digging, he would use his AK – 47 rifles to kill me or just put me into that hole and bury me alive.

While I was digging the earth, the super-natural happened. In the forest where I was digging, the big branch of a palm tree and palm fruits fell down and hit the local militia who was guarding me. He lost consciousness so I could escape. This was the act of God who constantly helped me behind the scene.

Democratic Republic of Kampuchea (DRK) - Khmer Rouge (KR) 1978
My Life in the Evil Khmer Rouge Regime

I was back to the different children's mobile team. Mit Bong and other base people's children constantly tyrannized new children including me. They kicked us. They slapped us and sometimes threw stones at us.

Angkar reduced food rations again. We, the new children received only a half cane of rice porite which is mostly rice porite's liquid and a half cane of water lily soup. Sometimes we received trokuon soup (water morning glory, a nutritious Khmer plant). During the DK regime, the food menu in all cooperative communities known as sahakor throughout the country was only rice porite's liquid and trokuon and pralit soup, or salt only.

On the other hand, the base people's children could have their own food both at home and at the cooperative community but not openly. Angkar gave them a priority with high privilege in everything. They had good food to eat at home and other benefits.

I planned to escape from my children mobile team stationed in Nang Sahet village to Smoung village. One day, after having lunch at the cooperative community, I went to a village near by known as Chapey village, located in the Tramkook district. I met one of the base people's children that I used to play with while I was living with my family in Smoung village. His name was Ath. I asked him about food rations. He told me in his village of Chapey, all children including people from all levels had enough food rations to eat at the cooperative community. I was shocked and asked myself why didn't Angkar allow us to have enough food rations to eat in Nang Sahet and other villages? Why was it completely different?

In the Pol Pot regime, people and children were divided into two classes: base people who used to live in a liberated zone and support Khmer Rouge during the war and new people, from provincial town and city.

I asked him if I could escape to live in his village. He said, "Yes, you can try". He continued, "I do not know what would happen to you". That afternoon, I did not return to work in Children's Mobile Team. I walked to the Chapey village cooperative community. Chapey village's Khmer Rouge militia messengers captured me. They tied me up with rope; tying both hands behind my back. They escorted me to the chief of the militia messenger's office. The chief of militia was known as comrade Sen. Comrade Sen asked me "Where did you come from"? I answered, comrade, "I do not know the name of the place where I came from. All I knew was that I came from a very far province," He continued questioning me "How did you arrive in Chapey village". I answered, "I was just walking by and just wanted to stop at this village to ask for some food rations to eat and if possible to live here since I do not have any family or relatives. I did not know where to go."

Comrade Sen ordered his militia to check immediately with the chiefs of villages near by i.e., Phum Se Chea, Phum Dan Kom, Phum Doeum Por and Phum Sdok. Comrade Sen said, "If you are lying, I will kill you." He kicked and slapped me. Then he said, "You are a liar. My militiamen found out that you have parents who live in our village. Tell me the truth."

I answered, "Comrade Sen, please, I do not have any family living here, in your village. If you find out my family lives here, you can kill me, now."

He said, "Let's see, Angkar has eyes and ears everywhere, like a pineapple's eyes known in Khmer as Angkar Pnek Mnoes"

Finally, Comrade Sen ordered his militiamen to release me. I was allowed to stay in Chapey village with the approval of the chiefs of the village and the militiamen. Chapey village's chief was a kind and good-hearted person. He was completely different from of his other comrades. I heard from the base people that he was one of Sihanoukist during the war against U.S imperialism. Most Khmer Rouge Sihanoukist are nice and kind to people. The radical Pol Potist is a mostly human killer. All people young and old including new and base people have enough food rations to eat in this village. This is the only village that I knew of under the Khmer Rouge regime where people had enough food rations to eat. Under the DK regime, local authorities including chiefs of village, commune, district and militiamen were very powerful.

I lived in Chapey village for nearly one month until in the midst of 1978. One day, I saw Mit Bong accompanied by militiamen from a distant come to our village and approach the community cooperative. I was terrified they would harm me. So I escaped to the forest near the village and continued my trip only at night to other village.

I am back to Smoung village again. I was allowed to stay at the village. The village offered very low food rations. I worked all day and night until 10:00pm. I collapsed again. My whole body and private area was swollen and I couldn't walk. I was suffering from malnutrition.

I was allowed to stay in the village, known as back battle line, with the base people who would bring me food rations from the community cooperative. Every day and night, I prayed God would save my life and all the other people's lives. I prayed God would send someone to help us out.

My whole body and private area continued to become more swollen. I knew that I would die soon. My body was very dirty. I

37

was covered with lice. My skin was rough and wrinkled and I looked like a ghost.

There were no medicines under the Khmer Rouge. Fortunately, I was helped by one of the daughters of the base people. She worked for the Khmer Rouge Army as a nurse's aid during her visits to their parents in the village. She injected fresh coconut juice into my body as IV solutions. Every other hour, she alternately injected palm tree juice. The base people gave me a natural effective medicine, coconut and palm juice to drink within a week. Day by day, my swelling went down all swollen spots ruptured and causing sores all over my body. If you pressed anywhere on my body including my private areas, you would see the surface was not normal. On the spot you pressed, it would have an indention, which would not return to normal. It would look like a big hole. Eventually, I got well again with the help of the nice base people. God helped me again and again through letting me meeting the good Khmer Rouge.

In the Khmer Rouge, this swollen disease was caused by malnutrition. It was happened through out the country. It was widespread in most people because, ninety five percent of people did not have enough nutritious food to eat. The disease killed thousands of people.

Angkar continued to teach children how to spy on our parents. Angkar told us our parents were not our real parents. Angkar was our real parent for all new and old children". Angkar also stressed that for new children, their own parents were the enemy of Angkar because they were the Angkar's destroyer and the CIA of the U.S imperialist.

Around thirty five percent of new children or even more numbers were brainwashed by Angkar. These children were forced to tell Angkar about their parent's background and way of life. Those children who told Angkar about their parent's occupation who used to work for Lon Nol, Khmer Republic Regime would be brought to revolutionary re-education and training. This means Angkar would kill them.

It is hard to imagine that not only children but also adult and all people through out the country, in Khmer Rouge Regime suffered from malnutrition, starvation, disease, poor living conditions, and illiteracy but it is true. Starvation was destroying the lives of not only children but also, youth, men and women through out the country. Under the Khmer Rouge Regime, there was little food or clothing for our people. Our people did not have even the basic necessities of life. People and children including myself focused on daily survival.

All people including children did not understand why the Khmer Rouge policy killed many of their own people.

Every day, I asked myself, why Angkar, the Group of Khmer Rouge Top Leaders including Pol Pot, Ieng Sary, Noun Chea, Khiev Samphan, Son Sen and others military and civil senior officials ordered the killing of their own people. First, they did not provide enough food rations. Second, they accused our people of working for the CIA and the supporters of U.S imperialists and other subversive activities.

Every day, under the Khmer Rouge, killing continued through out the country. The dead are piled up like mountains. If you were allow to walk from one village to another, you would see dead bodies everywhere in holes piled up like small hills.

It reminded me of stories that my uncle told me about how the communists are evil. They would kill every one even sometimes their own family. He told me that these top Khmer Rouge leaders were educated in Paris, France. In our society, we considered these educated people as dignified, highly ethical, moral and valuable people. They must know what is right and wrong. So why did these KR order this program of massive killing of its own people?

Every day, I cannot see any progress in this Khmer Rouge regime. What I saw was the fear, the killing, the starvation, the disease, the suffering and pain in every one of Cambodian's lives. Cars, trucks and motors were not moving like in the old days, when I was in Phnom Penh with my family.

As a child, I knew that I would die soon. It was just a matter of time. The Khmer Rouge will kill the children later, after they kill all of the old age people.

The KR claimed every day on radio broadcasting that they love the people. There is much progress and development under the rule of Angkar, Khmer Rouge. They continued to claim that under comrade Pol Pot's Leadership and his group, our society had no classes. Every one is equal. It is different from the Imperialist Lon Nol Regime. Angkar provides all the basic needs. The society has no classes like in the old regime. This was a completely lie. In fact, the Khmer Rouge regime turned Cambodia's history wheel backward, at least 30 years behind to do the reconstruction and redevelopment of all the country whole systems and infrastructures. The killing continued until 1979.

These Khmer Rouge leaders were more barbaric than Hitler. Hitler did not kill his own people. Hitler did things because he wanted to be a unique, powerful and superior nation in the world. So the ideologies are completely different.

Every day and night, I asked myself, why has Angkar killed so many people? Did the high organization "Angkar Leur" know this killing was happening? Of course, they did. They were the ones who ordered this massive killing. The Khmer Rouge accused that all new people from the cities and provincial towns are their enemy.

Without help from other countries, all the Cambodian people will be gone by Angkar's massive killing. Now, Angkar forced all of the new children including myself to leave their local concentration camp and moved to a different one faraway.

I asked permission from Mit Bong to leave to have a bowel movement in the open air. Taking this opportunity, I ran out of the camp into bamboo trees that were surrounded by the forest. I got stuck in there. I could not get out. When you're scared, the adrenaline can make you do things you couldn't ordinarily do. Finally, I was caught and forced to move to a station at Doeum Por village near Ant Mountain. Thank God, I met my older brother, Reagan by chance at the new camp but we pretended not to know or talk to each other. If the KR knew that we were brothers they would separate and move us to different camps.

Now, I was stationed in Doeum Por village near Ant Mountain. My life is better than before. My food ration was increased rice porite and soup. This year-end of 1978, all children's mobile concentration team members including myself, was trained to be in the Angkar army. We learned how to carry and use weapons.

The new chief of children's mobile concentration "Mei Kong" gave propaganda to all the children that the massive killing of the Cambodian people was done by the Vietnamese government. The KR claimed that the Vietnamese killed a lot of our people. This it was true as well. They said the Vietcong would kill you in many ways if you allowed yourself to be captured. One way was to cut a small hole in your stomach and put grass in it. Another way they said the Vietcong did this was to dig three holes then put a Cambodian in them. Then they put dirt over them leaving their heads sticking out as a holder for their stove to cook their tea. The Vietcong told the people in the hole not to move or they would spill their tea.

Angkar increased our food ration. Most of the children in the camp were scared of the Vietcong. As part of our children's job description, we were trained to be Angkar soldiers. All children's jobs including myself were much better than before. The new chief of the children's mobile concentration team Mei Kong told us that when you know all of the basic military tactics, Angkar would send you to the People's Republic of China for advanced military training.

Every night, after having dinner at the cooperative community, my brother, Reagan, and I secretly met together to discuss our life. I always climbed up a coconut tree to get coconuts. My brother kept a look out for any Angkar. After we got it we both secretly ate coconut and its juice. The concentration camp, where we were stationed was full of edible fruit trees. You could have it as long as Angkar did not see you do so.

At night, we made trips to the mountain to get sweet potatoes, French potatoes and other edible foods. We hid these foods in the forest or in the sandy land near our camp. One day, we both saw strangers, waving at us to approach them. But we were afraid and left the mountain immediately for our camp. We knew that they were the Vietcong military secret service or the spy. They had come here to see and evaluate the situation in the KR.

We did not tell Angkar about what we had seen. We knew that the Vietcong would attack the KR soon. Rumor spread within our camp that the Vietcong sent their military secret service to spy on Angkar so that they could attack.

This year was the year that the Khmer Rouge regime launched an attached Vietnam after the border negotiation was no solution. The Vietnamese government always says, "Yes" to agree on the borderline and treaty between the two countries which land is belong to Cambodia and which land belongs to Vietnam. But in reality, the Vietnamese moved in with forces and took our land and islands.

The new chief of the children's mobile concentration team Mei Kong gave propaganda repeatedly in the morning and in the evening before we were allowed to go to bed, that the Vietcong sent their military secret service to see the situation through out the country. Angkar said, they will attack us soon. Every day, Angkar updated us about the fighting in our land. Angkar also broadcast on the radio about their success in the fighting for our land in Kampuchea Krom. Angkar had control over part of our land in Kampuchea Krom. Angkar also claimed that they had killed many Vietcong. Angkar armies defeated the Vietcong troops. They continued that one Angkar soldier, could fight up to ten Vietcong soldiers. They continued that the top priority of Angkar was to get our land, Kampuchea Krom, back.

My friends in the camp including my older brother, Reagan and I knew that the Khmer Rouge regime would not last much longer. It is the rule of law and nature on earth that the evildoers will be destroyed at the end. Now may be the time that someone will come to help our country and us.

The Cambodian people in the whole country did not support the Khmer Rouge, Democratic Kampuchea government because this regime have killed many of their own people. They accused every one in the whole country was the enemy of Angkar. It was a rule of thumb, if the people do not support the evil government, the sooner or later it will be failed.

We, the children in the camp, wondered why now, at the end of 1978, Angkar seemed to take care of all of us. We knew that Angkar had killed thousands and thousands of children and its people. We knew Angkar is evil to their people. In the Khmer Rouge regime, there is no city. All people lived in the countryside and did farming.

We the children in the camp now seemed to see some bright light coming from the horizon. This meant that this regime, the KR would soon fall.

On the surface, society in Democratic Republic of Kampuchea was strictly egalitarian. The Khmer language, like many in Southeast Asia, has a complex system of usages to define speakers' rank and social status. These usages were abandoned. People were encouraged to call each other friend or comrade in the communist terminology way, and to avoid traditional signs of deference such as bowing or folding the hands in salutation. Language was transformed in other ways. The Khmer Rouge invented new terms. People were told they must forge a new revolutionary character, that they were the instruments of the Angkar, and that nostalgia for pre-revolutionary times or "memory sickness") could result in their receiving Angkar's "invitation."

As in other revolutionary states, however, some people were more equal than others. Members and candidate members of the Kampuchea Communist Party (KCP), local-level leaders of poor peasant background who collaborated with the Angkar, and members of the armed forces had a higher standard of living than the rest of the population. All Khmer people agree that, even during times of severe food shortage, members of the grass-roots elite had adequate, supplies of food.

The *damband* known as zone or region were divided into provinces, districts, subdistricts, and villages. The latter usually contained several hundred people. This pattern was roughly similar to that which existed under King Sihanouk and the Khmer Republic, but inhabitants of the villages were organized into groups composed of ten to fifteen families.

On each level, a three-person committee directed administration. Kampuchea Communist Party members occupied committee posts at the higher levels. Subdistrict and village committees were often staffed by local poor and uneducated peasants, and, very rarely, by new people. Cooperatives, similar in jurisdictional area to the *subdistricts*, assumed local government responsibilities in some areas.

Democratic Republic of Kampuchea (DRK)– Khmer Rouge (KR) 1979
My Life in the Evil Khmer Rouge Regime

While we, the children in the concentration camp were working in the morning and afternoon to dig the dam and canal to support the Youth and Mobile Team Concentration Camp. We saw hundreds and hundreds of KR troops, dressed in black uniform, with scarf, rubber sandals, and cap. Some carried rocket B-40 and others AK-47 rifles with sack of arms surrounded their body. They walked from the east toward the west where we were working. We knew that the Vietnamese troops invaded Cambodia to help us out.

There were two advantages for the Vietnamese invasion to Cambodia, the first thing, they can claim that they were here to help us out to survive from the evil Khmer Rouge who killed their own people and it is true. Second thing, they can take some of our land and island and natural resources and properties in returned.

The situation was chaotic. The new chief of the children's mobile concentration team, ordered us to leave work immediately. He told us that Angkar had a new order and we were to move back to the camp. We were sent to a meeting to receive new orders. Angkar said that the plan that all the children in our team would be sent to China for the military training was postponed due to the fact that there were lots of dark elements that Angkar had to take care of. He stressed that Angkar set this as the priority task. He also said Angkar would wait to see when it was a good time to send all of us to China either by ship or airplane. We needed to pack our belongings and move to work in another location near by the mountain to support Angkar soldiers. They continued to order us to move to the forest and up the mountain along with the Khmer Rouge armies.

On that day, we continued our journey until late night. We stopped by one of the villages near Sen Harn Mountain, which is located in Kampot province. The new chief of the children's mobile concentration team accompanied by his deputies, assistants and bodyguards asked the Khmer Rouge villagers for their rice, chickens and cows to make soup for all the children. The KR villagers refused him, but they were threatened and asked, "Why don't you obey Angkar? This was a crime against our revolution." He continued "By my order we, the Angkar, will take this any way".

We, the children were so happy with a mixed feeling of nervousness. We hoped that we would be able to eat that soup that we had never eaten before (in the Khmer Rouge Regime). We are all kind of reluctant and asked ourselves why is the KR being so nice to us at this time? They may kill us after they allow us to have this delicious food. The Khmer Rouge strategy is to sometimes before killing you people they allow you to eat, and then they kill you, later. Another reason is to force you to eat until you die. They knew that we could not eat much because our stomach and immune system was very weak and cannot hold a lot of food. If you never have enough food to eat all of your body systems become small.

The guards with the help of the big children tied the cow up. These guards took their sharp knife out of the sheath and pushed it into the cow's neck. The blood was flowing everywhere. Finally, the cow died. We had to help them butcher the cow.

Most of the children hid some of the beef including my brother and me. We knew in an advance that the situation was not normal. We must be ready to escape from the Khmer Rouge. All the children just looked at each other with wonder in their face. They whispered to one another about what was happening. We, the children knew that the KR soldiers or the Angkar's rule might collapse. They made delicious beef soup for all the children in the team.

While we stopped there, the Khmer Rouge soldiers continued their journey and marched up to the mountain. Fortunately, The Khmer Rouge soldiers left us behind.

On the next day, the new chief of the children's mobile concentration team was waiting for the order, but it seemed like their communication was cut off. We stayed at that village for about three days to receive the new order. On day three, we heard a loud artillery explosion near the village where we all were stationed temporarily. We also heard in the far distant east the sound of small weapons fire. Then, the sound became nearer. We all realized that the Vietnamese soldiers were coming toward us to liberate Cambodia.

On that day, the new chief of the children's mobile concentration camp team ordered us to a meeting after dinner. The Khmer Rouge gave each of us three kilogram of rice and some food, and then they dismissed us. The new chief of the children mobile concentration camp team was good Khmer Rouge. They told us that you could go to where ever you want. You can go to meet your family. Those whose do not have a family can go to see your relatives. You can go to whatever villages you come from. If he did not let us go, we might get stuck with Khmer rouge soldier and they might kill us if we did not follow their order.

All the children in our team were very happy that Angkar dismissed us. My brother and I had some beef and chicken to keep for our food. We both left all the children. We asked each other, where are you going? Most of them answered "I am going back to my former village where I stayed the first time when our family came from Phnom Penh, to find my parents" Each individual went on their own way to the villages where they came from. My brother and I with five other children were going to the same district, Angkor Chey.

We all talked how lucky our children's team was. The new chief of the children's mobile concentration team allowed all the children to go on their own. We saw other, children's mobile concentration teams, whose chief forced them to move along with the Khmer Rouge soldiers up to the mountain. In their team, if some one tried to escape and was captured, Angkar or the chief of their team would kill them.

That night, we saw artillery shells exploding everywhere. We were lying on the ground. We tried to find a safe place to hide. We saw the Vietnamese jet fighter bombing the mountain and the villages near the mountain. The mountain was on fire because of the bombs that dropped from the Mig 21. At night we could see clearly the light of the forest fire on the mountain.

My brother told me that through our military training, we knew that all the bombs; its shrapnel and bullets fired are flying through the air. Therefore to avoid them, we should get as low to the ground as we can.

The artillery shell and gunfire was exchanged between the Khmer Rouge soldiers and the Vietnamese armies. We heard the sound of "rack. ...rack...rack and then bomb bomb...". This indicated that the shells would fall close to us.

The next day, we continued our trip toward the national roads. The Khmer Rouge villagers told us that we were not allowed to travel. They told us if the KR soldiers saw us they might kill us.

We walked from village to village. We cooked rice with our old dirty port. We fried a small portion of chicken and beef for our meal. We were kind off worried because we knew our rice was going to run out. We stopped by different villages on our way to the national roads. We both asked the Khmer Rouge villagers "Comrade, please give us four or five canes of rice so that we can survive". They said "No". They continued, "All of you are new people, the 17th of April's people, we hate you. Get away from my face!"

We arrived in another village. We saw there were a lot of watermelons in the field. We wanted to pick one but it seemed there were a lot of people there. We held our position and looked around. We saw a couple in their late forties with two kids. The husband walked into the watermelon field and picked up two watermelons. Suddenly, the Khmer Rouge villagers and soldiers came out from the cottage and hit the man with a long sharp knife. His neck was cut in two and the blood spilled everywhere.

We were very sad that no one had the ability to help that man. The Khmer Rouge soldiers and its villagers killed the man. Oh, boy, these murderers killed people like killing an animal. The kids and the wife were crying for help and ran away from the scene because they feared they were next.

We including the new people were running away from the field too. We continued our trip but carried the horrible memory of what we saw. We feared for our own lives. In this world, how can people kill people just because of two watermelons?

We stopped at one place before continuing our trip toward the national roads. Gee, we saw there were a lot of people and children there from different mobile camps, villages, communes and districts. We searched around trying to look for our friends, relatives and family, Mom and youngest sister. Luckily, Reagan and I met Aunt Sang and my Cousin Stella and Marakot, there. We were all happy. We asked her if she had seen my mom, my youngest sister, Margaret and the rest of our family - Uncle Song and his children, Uncle Son and his children, Uncle Khak, Aunt Sar and her children, Aunt Sinh, Cousin Ang and Cousin Sung. She said "No, we have not seen any one of our relatives except you two."

After that, my other five friends who used to stay in the same children's mobile concentration camp said good-bye to us. We all started missing each other. One asked "How can we say good-bye". Reagan and I answered, "Just the same way we said hello the first time, we all met in the camp". They all said, Reagan and I were very lucky that you met your aunt and cousins. We were both sad to see our teammates walk away from us with a look of hopelessness and sadness on their faces. In each one of their minds, they wondered if they could find their parents, sisters, brothers and other relatives. They continued to wonder the same as we did, if our parents were still alive.

Reagan and I told Aunt Sang that we had some beef and chicken. She was very happy that she could cook good food for us that night. My Aunt Sang is very smart. She speaks French, English and Vietnamese. She was a teacher during the Khmer Republic Regime. Her husband was a military pilot and flew the T28. Unfortunately he was killed when communist anti-aircraft missiles hit the plane, leaving Aunt Sang a widow.

She laid out the plan that we all needed to do next. She said, first we have to walk toward the national roads to meet with the liberation armies. There, we would go to our former village Smoung, Samlang commune, Angkor Chey district which is located in Kampot province. We hoped to find out your mom, youngest sister and our uncles, cousins and aunts there. If we found them we might go back to Phnom Penh or Vietnam or Thailand, depending on the situation.

Now, Angkar was not in control of the situation. After having dinner together, we continued our trip toward the national roads. There we would continue to walk to Deoum Por village. Most of the Khmer people during the Khmer Rouge regime, around eighty percent of the population had an eyes disease called blind chicken know in khmer as "chomnhoer kwak moen". This eye disease caused you to have poor night vision or you cannot see at night.

After walking in the dark for about five hours, we arrived at the national roads. We were very happy to arrive there. Reagan and I asked Aunt Sang and her children to wait for us because we wanted to urinate in the forest. The Khmer Rouge was hiding in the forest. They put a lot of small tree leaves on their head and body to camouflage themselves. That way, they could ambush and attack any Vietnamese or liberation troops who passed by that area.

Reagan and I walked into the thin forest around seven or eight meters from the national roads to urinate. We stopped and started to urinate, and then the Khmer Rouge grabbed our private parts and said, "Are you blind? Aren't you? I would kill you if you urinated on my face". He ordered us "Go to the other side and do as you want to do".

We said, "Sorry, comrade, we both have blind chicken. Blind chicken was a disease in Khmer Rouge regime that people could not see at night when they have a blind chicken disease. We did not have any intention to do it on you, comrade, sorry". He continued, "Don't tell any one that we are here. We will kill you if we find out that you told people".

Aunt Sang was wondering why it was taking us so long just to urinate. She worried about our safety. After urinating, we returned to the national roads. Then we saw there were six Khmer Rouge soldiers with AK-47 and rocket B40 standing in the middle of the road stopping people. They asked a few questions: the first questions is "Where are you going?" second, "Where is your village?" third "Who is your chief?" and so on.

People saw there were only six Khmer Rouge soldiers on the road but in fact, there were around one hundred to two hundred Khmer Rouge soldiers hiding in the thin forest near the national roads ready to ambush any Vietnamese and liberation military tanks, trucks, troops that passed by this road.

Our turn came; Aunt Sang approached the Khmer Rouge. The soldiers asked, "Woman comrade, where are you going?" Aunt Sang replied, "We are going back to our village." They continued, "Where is your village?" She answered, "It is Smoung village, Samlang commune, Angkor Chey district. The KR said, "No, Angkar would not allow you to go back there for now because there were lots of dark elements that Angkar needs to clear and eliminate."

That night, we returned to the village near the national road and stayed there for the night. In the morning, we talked to the Khmer

Rouge villagers who lived there. They told us that the KR soldiers would allow you to return to your village if you came from the village near here. On that night, we went back to the national roads again. We were asked the same questions. Aunt Sang answered that we all came from Doeum Por village, near Ant Mountain. We continued our trip by walking for about sixty hours. Finally, we arrived in Doeum Por village.

We all lived in Doeum Por village for about one week. Aunt Sang insisted we go and find food. Reagan and I went out to find food. Aunt's Sang children, Cousin Stella and Marakot went out to find rice. Reagan and I went out fishing and crabbing.

While fishing, Reagan and I met one of our old friends, one of the five teammates who used to live in the same village and mobile concentration camp with us. He told us he had seen our mom in the village. We were both surprised and said, you must be kidding. He said, no, I am serious. If you do not believe me, I can take you there and show you where she lives. Then, Reagan and I said, yes, yes, we will give you some of our fish, if this is real. It turned out to be true. He took us to where our mother was. We gave him four of our fish. We met our mom, Kim Nang and our youngest sister, Margaret.

Reagan and I were so happy that we had a family reunion that afternoon. Now, we had to look for Uncle Khak, Uncle Song, Uncle Son" Aunt Sar and all our cousins. We found Uncle Khak, Aunt Sar and most of our cousins: Ang, Vireak, Vira, Veasna, Lundi, Dovine. They were all still alive, except for Uncle Song and Uncle Son who were killed in the bloodshed of the Khmer Rouge Pol Potist regime.

Mom told us that we had to go to Kampuchea Krom, which now belonged to Vietnam because we were afraid the Khmer Rouge might gain power again and kill us.

January 7th, 1979 is the date that half of the country was liberated by the Vietnamese Government with the support of the Cambodian resistance against the Khmer Rouge. The bloody Khmer Rouge regime had collapsed that day. There was lots of revenge against the chief of village, the chief of children and youth mobile concentration camp but also the base people who had killed the new people families and their children. Now, was the time for revenge and to fight back against the Khmer Rouge chief who had committed lots of killing against the new people.

In some villages, the new innocent people who had lost their family's lives during the Khmer Rouge regime because he had murdered the new people and their family hit the chief of the village with a sharp knife.

Our family was so angry. We had lost my father, three Uncles Song, Kru Kun and Son with seven cousins, one Aunt Sin. We wanted to find some one to help us to kill the chief of our former Smoung village who had ordered the militia men to take our father to the revolutionary re-education. Our father was never seen again. He was killed by the Pol Potist regime.

But Mom and Uncle Khak said, "Revenge is ignorance. It will continue without end, so please forget that. We cannot undo the death of our father and relatives even if we had an opportunity to take this evil man's life" (the chief of the village).

Mom continued "We have to think and prepare our lives for the future. Do not think about the past. We have to take the past as an experience. We learn from the past to avoid any wrongdoings and to improve on everything."

My family, Mom, sister, Reagan and I and Aunt Sang's family, Cousin Stella and Marakot walked along the national roads. On our way, we saw hundreds of Vietnamese military trucks loaded with valuable property from Cambodia being transported to their country. Mom spoke with these Vietnamese soldiers in Vietnamese and asked if they could give us a ride to Kampuchea Krom, the southern part of Cambodia, which currently occupied by Vietnam.

The French colonialists cut our Cambodian land, Kampuchea Krom, to the Vietnamese after the French withdrew from Indochina in 1951 and gave each country independence. Kampuchea Krom is now part of South Vietnam.

These Vietnamese soldiers were very nice. They said they could give us a ride. Our two families: my family and Aunt Sang's family with Uncle Khak and Cousin Ang were the first family to go to Kampuchea Krom.

When we arrived at the border between Cambodia and Vietnam, these Vietnamese soldiers asked us to get out of the military truck. They did not allow us to cross over on their truck into Kampuchea Krom, South Vietnam. We had to walk and cross the border illegally.

On our way, we saw that Vietnamese soldiers had moved the milestone boards, signs and fences, (built by the Khmer Republic regime to identify the border between the two countries) into Cambodian territory at Kabao, Moth Chruk and Phnom Den, at least four to five kilometer into Takeo province. It meant that the Vietnamese government had taken our land for five kilometer by using hardware, tractors and bulldozers to dig a small canal to separate the two countries.

Our uncles said, "Our Khmer leaders wage war against their own people and leave the country to be violated by foreign countries, i.e. the Socialist Republic of Vietnam and others." Unfortunately, it was sad that the Cambodian people never had good leaders who could stand up and rebuild our country toward inner peace, prosperity and harmony like western countries. The Khmer Rouge was one of the most evil and barbarous regime that killed millions of its own people. They turned Cambodia back at least 30 years behind in everything.

Aunt Sang and Uncle Khak said to just forget about that. There is nothing we could do about it. We were here to survive from the Khmer Rouge regime. Let's find something to eat. We stopped there. We were so happy to see lots of people, people on motorcycles, bicycles and cars moving around. We saw markets, restaurants, schools, good houses, and buildings everywhere. Mom bought us breads with delicious roast pig and Chinese soup to eat. We all were eating like people who came from another planet. Mom said you could eat what ever you want. Mom had to cut off her gold to sell it in a local market to get the Vietnamese currency that we could spend.

Aunt Sang sold her gold earrings for Vietnamese currency so that she could buy food and other things for her two lovely kids, Stella and Marakot. We were all so excited to see this. It reminded us of the old days, when we were living in the capital city of Phnom Penh, and the country was at peace.

Oh, boy, this is the first time in a long time that we could eat enough delicious foods. All of us saw foods; bread and Chinese noodle soup, which seemed like magic food that came from heaven. Thank God that He always watch over my family and me. We had food to eat now, but we still worried about our future. Mom and Aunt Sang talked about their personal valuable property. Mom and Aunt sang were kind of worried and sad, wondering what we were going to do when our gold property ran out.

After the fall of the Khmer Rouge regime in January 1979, The Vietnamese communist government took lots of valuable properties from Cambodia for example: gold, diamonds, silver, bronze (from the national sanctuary, treasury and museum), watches, cars, motorcycles, radios, TVs, raw rubber, rice, corn and other things and transported them to Vietnam. Every day, we could see hundreds of Vietnamese trucks loaded with these valuable items transported into Vietnam.

The Vietnamese government installed the new Cambodian government known as the National United Front for the Solidarity and Salvation of Kampuchea. After that they changed the name to the People's Republic of Kampuchea.

Our two families, my family, Aunt Sang, Uncle Khak and Cousin Ang arrived first in Kampuchea krom, now Vietnam occupied, to the small provincial town known as Nha Bang, We were very happy there. We were still waiting for the rest of our families to arrive here. We had our grand pa and grand ma from my mother's side who were living in Kampuchea Krom. Our main goal was to go and live with them for a while. While living with them, we learned about the situation in Cambodia both politically and economically to see if we could return and live in our native city, Phnom Penh. Every day, our uncles and aunts listened to the radio to learn if the Khmer Rouge regime had completely collapsed so that we could return to Cambodia.

My grandfather's name was Chau Nhep. He and parents was a Chinese immigrant from Manchuria in the north east of China. He immigrated to Kampuchea Krom when he was around sixteen, in 1920. He left years before the Japanese Emperor colonized Manchuria in 1934, which continued until 1945. Grand pa Nhep is a loud, open, honest man, sincere in friendship and quick in making decisions.

He then met our grandmother and married. They had eleven children, my mom, Kim Nang and her sisters: Kim Sang, Kim Sar, Kim Sin, Kim Choung, Kim Chhun, and her brothers: Kim Duth, Sokhak, Chau Song and Chau Son. He loves all of his grand sons and daughters equally.

Grandmother and grandfather felt sad to see all of us in such a poor health condition. Our immediate relatives including my mom, Margaret, Reagan and I were very skinny with the poorest health condition because we had no food to eat for nearly four years during the Khmer Rouge regime. This caused most of our young cousins including me to have stunted growth because of lack food and vitamin.

The People's Republic of Kampuchea (PRK)
January 7th, 1979
My Life in Another Communist Regime (PRK)

After the Vietnamese invasion, the Khmer Rouge (KR) regime, fell on January 7, 1979. The same year, the Hanoi Vietnamese Government installed a new Cambodian government known as the National United Front for the Salvation of Kampuchea, later, People's Republic of Kampuchea led by President Heng Sam Rin and Prime Minister Pen Sovann. Mr. Pen Sovann was also a commander in chief and Defense Minister for PRK regime. The advantage of the Vietnamese invasion in Cambodia was that it provided help for the Khmer people to survive from the Genocidal Khmer Rouge regime. The disadvantage was that part of our territory, country was taken by the Vietnamese government (VG) and our entire country was under their control and colony. They (VG) moved their border at least from five to ten kilometers into Cambodia. They also took our islands, "Koh Pulowaii". It means that we not only lost our land at least ten kilometers all along the eastern border but also our islands. Most of our national treasures, valuable properties were also taken and transported to Vietnam. There was millions of Vietnamese illegal flowing and residing into Cambodia. The PRK government has to give them a privilege in everything in exchange for their support and long lasting power.

Kampuchea-Krom means "Cambodia Below" or "South Cambodia". In ancient times Kampuchea-Krom was the southern territory of the Khmer Empire, and later it was known as (French)

Cochin China. It is now the southwestern part of Vietnam. It covers an area of some 89,000 km² with Cambodia to the north, the Gulf of Thailand to the west, and the South China Sea to the southeast and the Champa's territory to the northeast. Prey Nokor was one of the most important commercial cities of all in Kampuchea-Krom, but the name was first changed to Saigon and then to Ho Chi Minh City by the Vietnamese Communist in 1975. This had been our land, which was cut up by the French colony government, and given to Vietnam after World War II, 1945-1949.

It is estimated that there are about 8 million Khmers living in Kampuchea-Krom. Approximately 80 percent of them live in the Mekong delta, and a small number are in other provinces throughout the southern part of Vietnam. Besides the Vietnamese, there are other ethnic people living in Kampuchea-Krom, including Chinese, the Chams, the Mountgards, and many other small ethnic groups.

While living in Kampuchea Krom, Svay Tong near Kaboa Math Chruk (now it's south Vietnam), we, our families studied the political and economic situation in the Cambodia and countryside so that we could decide if we could return and live in Phnom Penh, our native city. Every day, our Uncle and Aunts listen to the radio to learn about the Khmer Rouge regime and see if they had failed 100 percent so that we could return to Cambodia.

At this time, the local Vietnamese government ordered all Cambodians who lived in Kampuchea Krom known as Khmer Krom (mostly the people were of two citizenships: Vietnamese and Cambodian) to leave their home and property. Grandpa and Grandma said, "This land and home are our land and our home. Why can't we live on our own land and in our own home?"

Cambodia has many sufferers. Those who lived in Cambodia suffered and many were killed by the Khmer Rouge. The Khmer Krom who lives in Kampuchea Krom, (the Cambodian land that the French Colony cut up and gave to the Vietnamese) suffered, were tyrannized and killed by the Vietnamese government. We all suffered great pain from these two evils, the Khmer Rouge (KR) and the Vietnamese communist government (VG).

So now where is the place that our family and all other Cambodian should go??? Like the proverb says, "We escaped from the crocodile in the water only to be in the land of the tiger." ("chooh tek kra poe leoung leu kla.")

Therefore, our grandma, grandpa and the rest of our family were forced by the local Vietnamese authority to abandon their home and properties. Grandma, grandpa and the rest of our family was forced to evacuate to Totim district, svay chrum commune in Kleng Province (named during the Khmer Empire) and later the Vietnamese changed the name and it is now known as Huao Yang Province. We were ordered to bring nothing along. If we did the local Vietnamese government would punish us. Grandpa and grandma lost their home, land and all personal property.

With the support of Khmer-Krom there, Grandpa, grandma and our family settled down. There, my brother, Reagan, cousin, Stella and I were registered to study in the Vietnamese elementary school. I also studied Khmer literature in the Entekorsey pagoda "Wat Entekorsey", which was taught by a Khmer Krom monk.

At that time the Vietnamese government started recruiting Khmer Krom people to work in Cambodia because most of our intellectuals were killed by the Pol Potist regime. Time flies so fast. Now it was 1980. My brother, Reagan, Uncle Khak, Aunt Sang and her two kids-Marakot and Stella, Aunt Sar and her five children decided to leave Kampuchea Krom for Phnom Penh with the recommendation of our grandpa "Chau Nhep" for hopefully a brighter future. They all arrived in Phnom Penh, the capital city of Cambodia, in May 1980.

There, Uncle Khak, Aunt Sar and Aunt Sang registered with the new Cambodian government, the People's Republic of Kampuchea. Through their individual background, Uncle Khak, a pharmacist, was assigned to be the Head of Monk Medical Hospital "Munti Pet

Luk Sarng". Aunt Sar and Aunt Sang were assigned to be teachers in Bak Touk School, Phnom Penh.

My mother, Margaret and I stayed in Kampuchea Krom till 1981. On March 20, 1981, with the recommendation of our grandpa, we left there and arrived in Phnom Penh on March 28, 1981. We were arriving in Phnom Penh late because new owners had occupied most of our house.

My mom went to our former house where I spent the first five years of my childhood. Unfortunately, after liberation day on January 7th 1979, whoever came first, to live in any house or property became the legal owner. There was no legal document that would be recognized by the People's Republic of Kampuchea. Then, Mom went straight to Uncle Song's villa, which we all left in 1975. Now the Vietnamese high-ranking officials known as Vietnamese Military Experts lived in this beautiful villa. Mom spoke in Vietnamese asking their permission to see the villa. She negotiated with a Vietnamese Military Expert to share the treasure of diamonds and gold that belonged to our family. We had hidden it in 1975 before we were forced to leave the city.

Finally, they came to an agreement of a 70/30 split. I mean they were to get 70 percent of the gold and diamonds of our family's treasure and we were to receive 30 percent of it. They allowed Mom to see the house and to tell them where the treasure was. Some treasures were hidden in the yard and some in the water tank (basin), which is located on the top of the villa. After digging up the yard and diving into the tank, they found the treasure. They gave my mom nothing. They were evil. They did not keep their word but accused Mom of being a Pol Potist. Mom pleads for her life and got nothing more. Because mom could speak Vietnamese finally they released her.

Under the People's Republic of Kampuchea's regime, if they (the Vietnamese military experts or a communist organization) wanted to tyrannize or kill anyone, they accused them of being a Pol Potist.

Mom was so sad that day because she lost everything and could easily have been killed. She said she had to live because all of us-Reagan, Margaret and I, needed her so badly. Thank God that the Vietnamese military expert spared her life.

Mom was a self-employed businesswoman. First she traded gold from Vietnam to Cambodia. Later, she traded medicine from Vietnam to sell in Cambodia.

Both, my sister Margaret and I were now living in Phnom Penh with Aunt Sang. Reagan was living with Uncle Khak. Mom went to Vietnam regularly by boat to buy medicine and sell it in Cambodia. When business was getting very tough, mom decided to stop. Every one of her trips took around four weeks for her to be back home in Phnom Penh.

Margaret and I registered for the second grade in Bak Touk School. Reagan was in fourth grade at the same school. We were all so excited to have an opportunity to study and to be in the same school was wonderful. We could see each other every day. Margaret and I studied in the class, which was taught by Aunt Sang.

At the end of 1981, the government banned all private business. Mom was forced to close her business down. There is only one business in the country and it was run by the state, the People's Republic of Kampuchea. The government ran everything including all of the shops and stores. The government employees had no salary. They worked to exchange food to survive.

The way that the People's Republic of Kampuchea ran the country was quite similar to the Khmer Rouge Regime. You could not travel from one place to another without permission from the local authority. There was no private employer. The government employs all employees. They did not have a salary. Food was offered at its own collective community, later year they started having salary.

At the end of November 23, 1981, one of the top leaders of People's Republic of Kampuchea, Mr. Pen Sovann, the defense minister, Secretary General of the Cambodian Communist Party, and Prime Minister, was arrested by the Vietnamese government with secret plot and jealousy against him by his own politburo committees which include Heng Sam Rin, Say Bou Thoung and Hun Sen because he refused the order from the Hanoi government to give part of Cambodian land to Vietnam and not allow illegal Vietnamese people to live in Cambodia and also some other border, political issues and especially he preferred to have a direct relationship with the former Soviet Union not through his foreign ruler. Mr. Pen Sovann is known as a good leader and a peacemaker harmony and prosperity loving person. He loves his people and country. He has a strong national interest. He is a man of good hearted and a loving people.

During his interview, Mr. Pen Sovann said "he got an order from the Hanoi Vietnamese government not to nominate Mr. Hun Sen. Mr. Hun Sen will be nominated directly by the order of Vietnamese government to be the Cambodian foreign minister and Vietnamese right hand man in the PRK regime. Mr. Hun Sen is the eyes and ears for the PRK regime and for his foreign ruler, Vietnamese. He continued that after his official military trip from the western province, Battambang to be the economic zone, when he arrived home in Phnom Penh, near Chamcar Mon, former Khmer Republic Presidential Palace, there was lot of Vietnamese military tanks surrounding his home. And the Vietnamese guards replaced his military national guards. After taking off, he knew that something was wrong. But he decided to walk straight with his comrade to play badminton and also to observe the situation near by; Vietnamese guards followed him".

Forty-five minutes later, he returned home and the Vietnamese guards were still following him. He picked up the phone and called his General Meas Sophea and asked who send the military tanks to surround his home, the answer was "Bon, I don't know". When people called you "Bon" is to show his respect. Then he started calling his interior minister, Mr. Chea Sim and asked the same questions, the answer was " Bon, I don't know".

A few minutes later, he saw his foreign minister; Mr. Hun Sen with his politburo member, Say Bou Thong and their Vietnamese ruler secret services walked up to his villa and slam his table. Mr. Hun Sen said, "Bon, you are a traitor and you are too nationalist", then he pulled out a small paper from his jacket and read: We, the politburo committees decided:

1. Bon Pen Sovann did not allow illegal Vietnamese to live in Cambodia. We, our people of Cambodia also live in Vietnam during the war and the Khmer Rouge time. Bon Pen Sovann is too nationalist.

2. Bon Pen Sovann charged the fees for when the Vietnamese ruler airplanes landing in the Cambodia Pochengton International Airport without understanding that we, the two are fraternal countries.

3. Bon Pen Sovann did not respect the decision of our foreign ruler, the Vietnamese.

Base on the above mistakes, we, the politburo committees decided to dismiss Bon Pen Sovann from his position, started immediately. Then, his foreign minister knocked out the table and walked out. Later the foreign ruler secret services slab him in the face of his sunglass, Ray Ban and hand caught him, thrower him into the military truck and drove him away to Pochengton International Airport. Later, they flew him to be prison in Hanoi, the socialist republic of Vietnam.

During that time, Hun Sen was the minister of foreign affairs. Later, he was promoted by the Vietnamese Government to be Deputy Secretary General of the Cambodian Communist Party, and became the Prime Minister. Heng Samrin was the president of the People's Republic of Kampuchea. Hun Sen was the Vietnamese right-hand man in the People's Republic of Kampuchea's government. He and his comrades- Heng Samrin, Say Bouthorng, Bou Thorng and etc. would do everything to satisfy his foreign master, the Vietnamese, because of the power. Mr. Hun Sen and his group was the one who secretly plot an arrest against his boss, Mr. Pen Sovann, Prime

Minister and Defense Minister with the collaboration of his Vietnamese military experts.

To keep the People's Republic of Kampuchea regime from collapse, there were around between 200,000 to 300,000 (three hundred thousand) Vietnamese troops in the Cambodia between 1979 and early 1991. The Khmer Rouge moved to the western part of the country, near the Thai border. They started resisting and fighting against the People's Republic of Kampuchea. The Vietnamese troops and military experts were everywhere in the country. They were in all government ministries. In every ministry and organization, there were Vietnamese military experts to run and manage them and they were the rulers of the Cambodian Ministers. The Cambodian ministers and senior official has no authority to do everything without an approval from his ruler counter part, the Vietnamese.

With this kind of situation, every day it was getting more difficult. Aunt Sar, Aunt Sang and my mom were talking together to find a way to escape to Thailand in order to become refugees in a third country. I mean western countries like the USA, France, Australia, Germany and so on.

One night, Aunt Sang and mom talked of how Aunt Sang would leave Phnom Penh on Saturday of the next week to go to the Thai border through Battambang province and Svay Sisophon. She asked my mom whether she would like to go with her. Mom was kind of reluctant. She said, "We have to cross land mines, the Khmer Rouge Zones and other obstacles". Then mom decided not to go at this time. But she asked Aunt Sang to take my brother, Reagan along with her. So, there would be four of them, Aunt Sang, her son, Stella and daughter, Marakot and Reagan going.

Saturday came. Reagan got up late. He came from Uncle's Khak apartment and arrived at Aunt Sang's apartment late. So, Aunt Sang and her two children left without him. They went to board the train at 5:00 a.m. for Battambang province. Reagan went to the train station but unfortunately, he could not find Aunt Sang and the train left.

One month later, we heard that Aunt Sang had arrived at Kao-E-Dang camp in Thailand. Aunt Sar talked with Mom again. She tried to convince my mom to go along with her. Mom said, "If we meet the Khmer Rouge soldiers, our whole family will be killed". The fear for our lives and many other obstacles made mom decide not to go.

Aunt Sar with her five children left Phnom Penh for Kao Dang camp, Thailand. Fortunately, they all arrived at Kao Dang camp safety.

My Mom had sent Uncle Kim Duth to continue his education in France before the fall to the Khmer Rouge in 1975. He got his Ph.D. in Economic Sciences from Paris University, France and immigrated to live in Canada after the country's fall in the evil communist in 1975. He was the one who sponsored our whole family to immigrate to Canada. He filed the immigration applications for all of our family and sent our family list to the Thai refugee camp, with UNICEF and other Humanitarian and Charity Organizations who worked in Thailand. Fortunately, we had Uncle Duth to sponsor us. If not. There would have been great difficulty to find someone or organizational charities to sponsor our family to live in a third country.

At the end of 1981, we heard from Aunt Sang that every individual in our family had their name on the list in the Thai refugee camp, Kao-E-Dang. As soon as we could get there, we would be able to go to live in Canada.

We all now were facing difficulties to travel from Phnom Penh to the Thai refugee camp, Kao-E-Dang. We had to hire the Khmer military who is honest to take us across Cambodian border to the Thai Border and from there, we have to hire the Thai military to take us to Kao-E-Dang. This involved risking our lives and our personal belongings.

Most of the smugglers are members of the military, the police, or people who has connection with authorities and know the way there. The smugglers charged from one to three Damloeung of gold which is equal to from 400 to 1,200 U.S dollar per person but everything was negotiable. We had to cross many check points and the deep jungles full of land mines and high risk. We had to cross three major obstacles which involved the danger of lives: the People's Republic of Kampuchea (PRK) zone, then Khmer Rouge (KR) zone and finally to Thai soil or Zone, Kao-E-Dang. Khmer communist (PRK) who are in favor of Vietnamese and the Vietnamese controlled the PRK zone. The Khmer Rouge zone was one with a history of the most evil and bloodshed. Finally, the Thai army and Thai soil was the one who has heart of evil, not all.

According to Aunt Sang, "Most of the Khmer refugees who arrived at the Khmer-Thai border early in 1980, it was estimated that around fifty trucks were forced back to Cambodian soil by the Thai military. The Thai military throw them away back into the Cambodian soil. This first group was mostly tortured first by the Thai military and second killed by land mines, the Khmer Rouge who was stationed along the Thai-Cambodian border. Others were killed by the land mines and by the Thai soldiers for those who tried to escape back into Thai soil".

The People's Republic of Kampuchea (PRK) 1982-1983
My Life in Another Communist Regime (PRK)

Before Aunt Sang left for Kao-E-Dang Camp in Thailand, she had given Mom her apartment, known as Number 124E2, Bloc Seng Thai, St.109 that was located on the second floor. The three of us, Mom, my sister, Margaret and I were living in that apartment. Most of the people who lived in this complex were doctors, pharmacists, nurses, and government employees working for the Ministry of Public Health. We could live there because Uncle Khak was the Head of Monk Hospital "Munti Pet Luk Sanh". He later was demoted to Chief Bureau Technique, under the First Kampuchean Pharmaceutical Manufacture.

My Mom was working very hard just to feed the three of us. To release her burden, she asked Uncle Khak to help her in taking good care of and feeding our brother, Reagan. Now approximately at the end of 1981, Uncle Khak was married to a woman who worked in the same Ministry but a different department. My brother, Reagan, was living with them. We hardly ever saw each other in school because of different class programs and schedules. Even so, we still enjoyed studying because we had never had this kind of special opportunity before during the Khmer Rouge regime.

In the middle of 1981 or we can say at the end of 1980, the People's Republic of Kampuchea's Government printed currency known as "Riel" to spend throughout the country. Now, most of the government employees had some salary plus 20 kilograms of rice or up to 40 kilograms per month per individual or family. This provision was given according to the person's rank and occupation.

Mom told us that since she did not have any valuable properties to give to us, we must study very hard. She said education and knowledge is everything like the saying, "The thieves can steal your own valuable property but not your knowledge." School started at 7:00 AM and finished at 3:00 PM. At that time Mom did not have any regular income. She spent some of her savings that she had made while she did business during the past two years.

My brother, Reagan was promoted from the 4th grade to 7th grade. He was no longer in our school. He moved to Toul Kork High School. Every day, after school, I saw Mom was so sad. We, my sister, Margaret and I, were sad too when we saw this kind of situation. Every day Mom did her best to buy clothes from the government clothes store and tailor them for those who needed and wanted them. This is how Mom made our living.

The government began conducting security screenings to find those who had a background related to imperialism. What I mean are those people who had family relatives living abroad, for example in America, France or other western countries or the people who used to work for foreign governments or agencies. All people were classified into three categories:

- Class One: Communist Officials who had a pure background and rank known as "Kama PhiBal", "Pak Kchun" and, "Snol" respectively. This group also included those Khmer communist officials who married Vietnamese revolutionary women during the war that the communist called against U.S imperialism. This communist individual was considered as a senior official, official of the party, reserve official for community party with the title called "Kama Phibal", "Pak Kchun" and, "Snol" respectively.

- Class Two: The simple public employee or person who had a good background not related to imperialism.

- Class Three known as Three Hundred Fifty One Group: "351" for those people who had had their family work for foreign governments or had family members living in western countries, or their background related with different ethnicity, that is to say with half-blood of any races i.e. Chinese-Khmer.

The procedure that the (PRK) developed for the children was like this: when children whose parents were "Kama Phibal, "Pak Kchun" and, "Snol" were between the ages of six to thirteen, they were selected to be vanguard children. When these vanguard children grew to the age of fourteen to eighteen, they were known as communist youth. Then after college graduation or when they started working, first they have the title of Snol. Snol is the lower first title for communist party rank. If they were promoted they would become Pak Kchun. Pak Kchun is the person of the party of the second title, higher than Snol. Finally, Kama PhiBal was the high title for senior communist officials in the party.

Therefore if you were a young boy who had a dream to be a man in high position in the communist government, you first had to have a good family background, either in class one or class two so that, you can go ahead to the top. In addition, you had to pass through the stages of a vanguard child, communist youth (when you were in primary or secondary and high school), Snol, Pak Chrun and finally Kama Philbal (when you started working for the communist party, in any ministry or organization.

Under the People's Republic of Kampuchea (PRK) regime, students were not allowed to study western foreign languages, like English and French because these languages, the communist considered as imperialistic. Teachers, professors and students were punished if they studied or taught these languages.

In public school, there were two main foreign languages that the government had in the academic program: the first was Vietnamese as the top priority language, then Russian as the second priority language that needed to be studied.

Even though this was the law, there were many people still learning English and French in secret. Mom also encouraged us to learn French and English. I started to study English three hours per week on the weekend. In my English class, there were eight of us, three boys, Virak nickname, Poeun, Kheang and me, along with five adults, three men and two women.

Poeun was my next-door apartment neighbor. Both of our families were very close to each other. We both played together during our childhood. I always walked with Poeun back and forth to English school. On our way to school, we passed by Kheang's apartment. There, we stopped for a while waiting for Kheang. We sometimes called him from the ground and sometimes he was already waiting for us at the corner of Monivong, off the former USSR Boulevard. Then, we all matched together to school. It took us around ten minutes to arrive at our English class. The class was from 12:30 PM to 2:00 PM on the weekends. Our teacher was a woman. She used to work for International Organizations and the United States government agencies in Phnom Penh during the Khmer Republic, Lon Nol regime. She earned her Bachelor's degree from Phnom Penh University. She was a beautiful, smart and intelligent woman. She taught us using a British English book, known as "Essential English, Book One". This book has four in the series, going from book one to four.

Every time we had a class, the three of us took turns to watch out to see if there was any irregularity outside. It was on Saturday afternoons, my teacher asked me to go out and notice if there was any unusual activity or policemen around her apartment compound. This was the way we did when we had a class just to check if the local authority knew that we studied English there. We did this to avoid any arrests or captures.

The three of us were the youngest in the class. Therefore, my teacher assigned this task to us and we each had our turn. She knew that the local authority did not pay too much attention because we were very young.

Our English class went very well for about three months, till March 1982. One day, Kheang told Peoun and me that he would not be able to study English with us any more because his family was to escape secretly for the Thai border. They would live in a refugee camp so that they could go to live in a western country.

After the class, Kheang told the teacher about this. She told him in return "I might meet you and your family there." She wished Kheang the best of luck. We all walked back to our apartment. We were kind of sad that Kheang would leave us. We arrived at the corner of Kheang's apartment. We hugged each other and said, "How do we say goodbye?" Kheang smiled and replied, "Just as we say hello". Then we left each other with the feeling of a heavy-heart.

A month later, my English teacher told me that her family was planning to escape from Phnom Penh, PRK government to live first in the refugee camp in Thailand, then continue on to Australia. She asked me if my Mom would allow me to go with her family. She considered me as her child.

After the class on that day, I went straight home with Poeun. I asked Mom if I could go first to the refugee camp, then from there through the sponsorship of her family I could go to Australia with my English woman teacher's family. Mom said, "No," that she was concerned about my safety because I was very young. I told Mom that as soon as I got there, I could go to Canada because Uncle Kim Duth had already sponsored all of the members on Mom's side of the family.

Reagan, Margaret and I told Mom that we had a dream to live in a western country. Especially America. We all missed the chance in 1975. Will we miss this chance again? Every day, Reagan, Margaret and I blamed Mom for her big mistake of not leaving the evil communist regime before the fell of the Khmer Republic, supported by the U.S government to live in a western country.

We hardly had enough food and rice to eat because Mom's business was down. Mom was always trading her gold for food so that we could survive.

Mom said, "Definitely, Yes, I want to go. But there are many obstacles, landmines, the PRK communist, the Khmer Rouge, the Vietnamese troops and the Thai armies." Then, she cried, "Definitely, Yes, I want to go, but I do not want all of you to be killed by these evils. They can arrest you and force you to be in the army and kill your own people. And they killed you. Don't you understand?"

One month later, Uncle Khak's family including my brother, Reagan escapes to the Thai border refugee camp with the assistance from a smuggler. The smuggler cheated our family. They all were separated in Svay Sisophan, western Cambodian district near the Thai border. The smuggler reported to the local authority that Uncle Khak's family were imperialists who betrayed their country and wanted to escape to a western country.

Fortunately, Uncle Khak's family, which included his wife, two children and Reagan, escaped from the local authority safely. Reagan and Uncle Khak's family were separated. Uncle Khak's family arrived in Phnom Penh safely, but he was accused and charged by his communist officer, of the crime of betraying his country because of having the intention to leave the country. He and his family were forgiven of the crime because they were able to bribe the minister of public health.

The militiamen who were stationed in the district because he didn't have a letter of permission to travel arrested Reagan, on his way to back to Phnom Penh. Reagan wanted to run from them but the militiamen opened fired with their AK 47 riffles toward him. Fortunately, all the bullets were missed. They also found that Reagan had a note with a list of addresses in English. They charged him as a traitor to the country and for being a secret agent of imperialist with intentions against the communist regime.

A week later, the unidentified military, the police, came to our apartment and told Mom that Reagan had been arrested. They accused him of the crime of betraying his country of being a secret agent for imperialist country and revolution due to his intention to escape from the country and live in a western country.

Mom suddenly looked pale with fear. She asked personally to speak to the commander in private. She asked if he could help Reagan to get back to Phnom Penh. The man replied that his division was stationed there and he could help Reagan to get out. But that he would need one domleoung of gold, which equals four hundred and fifty U.S. dollars to take care of this case.

Mom tried to negotiate with him and said, "Please help my lovely son out, I have only three chi and a half of gold" which equals one hundred and forty five U.S dollars. The man said, "No, I have to have the total amount so that I can help him out. If not, your son will be in prison." Mom started crying and said, "Please help my son out, you are the commander in that area, you have the authority to release him. Please forgive him. He is young. He knows nothing about the revolution. I will educate him not to do this any more. I promised."

The man, then, seemed to have sympathy toward Mom and said, "Are you sure, you have only this amount?" Mom said, "Yes, sir that's the only amount I save to feed my children." He left and said, "Please do not tell anyone about this, even the group of police." That evening the whole family was sad, fearful and worried about Reagan's destiny.

Through the arrangement from the local military commander, Reagan was brought up to Kampong Chhnang province, around 75 kilometers from Phnom Penh. Mom had to ask permission from the local authority to travel to get Reagan back home.

A week later, we saw Reagan return home. He looked dark, skinny, pale, nervous, fearful and so dirty. He looked like a lost person because the militiamen had tyrannized him. He told us that the militiamen had opened fire with their AK-47 toward him and on the ground across both his legs to stop him. They did a lot of evil to him. Fortunately, the bullets did not hit him. Thank God, that they spared his life.

After this incident, our family had other problems. An attempt was made to force us out from our apartment. The high authority told Mom that we were not allowed to live in our apartment, the Bloc Seng Thai because this apartment complex was only for those who are high ranking communist officials known as "Kama Phibal".

Mom had bribed them by giving them her valuable personal property. But they still insisted us that we had to leave within forty-eight hours. If not, the military and police will come and take our belongings and we will be thrown in jail. Mom discussed this serious issue with Uncle Khak. He told Mom that he was not in a position to help out because the high authority was his boss.

Uncle Khak encouraged us to give our apartment to the high authority. We, Reagan, Margaret and I said "No, Where are we going to live if we give our apartment to the high authority?"

We, the three of us, decided not to leave our apartment. If the military and police come, let them kill us. If we can survive through the Khmer Rouge, why can't we survive in the PRK regime??

Mom tried to find support from different places but no one could help her. I told Mom that we had our cousin Ang who worked for the military department as a medical officer who could help us. Mom thought that he had left the country to the refugee camp for Canada already. She said, "If we go and ask for him, they might arrest us because we are his relatives."

On that night we all exchanged ideas with each other to find a solution. I said we needed to check if cousin Ang was still working there. The next day, we went to the military department and asked for cousin Ang. Fortunately, he was still working there. He told us that his plan of running out of the country was not successful. But he was planning to try again within the next 3 months when he would be assigned to work in the military base near the Thai-Cambodian border.

He said, he would talk to his commander, to help us out but he needs something to give him in return if he could help us. Finally, his commander agreed to talk to the high authority of ministry public health.

This problem was quiet for a while, so it seemed like they came to an agreement.

A couple of months later, the second, ministry of public health authority was threatening us. Every time the authority saw Mom, she said, "You have to leave comrade woman if you want to be safe. If not, we, the authority will take your apartment by force and harm you and your children."

Now the new high authority was our neighbor who wanted our apartment for his relatives. Mom started to explain to them the reasons why; we cannot give up this apartment because we do not have another place to live. Base on the PRK law and regulation, the people who first come and live in any apartment, property or houses after the liberation day, 7th January 1979 from the Khmer Rouge, that property, apartment or house legally belongs to that individual or family.

So finally, by the PRK law this apartment property belongs to our family. Mom told the authority that was our neighbor, "I need to have an official letter signed by the communist minister of public health stating that my family has to give this apartment to the high authority".

Mom tried her best to get support. She decided to give her valuable personal properties, gold to the high authority that was our neighbor to stop this problem. Mom prayed every day and night and finally the authority did not give us any more problems.

Now, we were facing starvation again. We didn't have enough food to eat. We had only one set of clothes. We wore them again and again. They started wearing out. Mom had to fix them for us. She sewed and covered each spot that was wearing thin. Our shirt and pants had more than ten pieces of cloth, covering spots that mom fixed for us.

Life in these two communist regimes had similarities and was not very different. But the PRK was much better than the Khmer Rouge. The PRK regime did not kill their own people directly like Pol Pot did. But it seems like they did in a different way or we can say, "PRK killed their own people indirectly, they let them die of starvation and hunger or by sending them out to be an open-wall of revolution against the Khmer Rouge resistant." These people were in middle between the government, the Vietnamese troops and the Khmer Rouge resistance forces.

The People's Republic of Kampuchea (PRK) 1983-1984
My Life in Another Communist Regime (PRK)

At this time Margaret and I were in the 4th grade of Bak Touk School. Reagan had moved to Toul Kork High School where he was attending 7th grade. In the early part of 1984, Margaret and I passed the exam and start attending 5th grade in the junior high school of Bak Touk. Reagan was then attending 8th grade in the same high school. We all loved to study! Every day, we dreamed of going to school because this presented a great opportunity to us.

The People's Republic of Kampuchea (PRK) received higher educational assistance from socialist countries, which included the former Soviet Union, East Germany, Bulgaria, Hungary, Poland, Czechoslovakia, India, Cuba, Mongolia and Vietnam. East Germany, Bulgaria, Hungary, Poland and Czechoslovakia were classified as number one countries. They were called "Class A" and were considered to offer the best quality not only in education but also student standards of living higher than the other countries. The former Soviet Union and Cuba, was considered country number two or "Class B". India, Mongolia and Vietnam were classified as number three countries, which was "Class C," the lowest category. Most students were concerned not only about the quality of education in a country but were also aware that number three, or "Class C" countries were not as good as "Class A" or "Class B" regarding the standard of living for students.

The procedure to apply for a scholarship to study in these socialist block countries was as follows:

Each student had to be sponsored by his or her parents and relatives who were classified as:

- Class One: Communist Officials who have pure backgrounds and are high ranking officials, either civil or military, known as " Kama PhiBal", "Pak Kchun" or "Snol".

- Class Two: The simple communist public employee or an employee who has a good background, not related to imperialism.

If Class "One" sponsored you, you had an excellent chance to receive a scholarship and you could choose the best country and the subject you wanted to study. If Class "Two" sponsored you, your chance of receiving a scholarship was around twenty five to thirty percent, depending on the connections of your family.

- Class Three: (known as the Three Hundred Fifty One Group "351") These were people who had no family working for the government; had family members living in western countries, or their ancestors was of a different ethnicity (e.g. Chinese-Khmer), or their family members were pure peasants or farmers.

If you were sponsored by Class Three, your chance of getting a scholarship was very slim or none. Maybe around three to four percent. In such cases, parents or relatives had to bribe the local educational authority for their son or daughter to receive a scholarship. The amount of the bribe depended on the class of the country being applied for. A scholarship to a "Class A" country could cost about three Dom Leoung of Gold, which equals one thousand four hundred ($1400) U.S Dollars. A "Class B" scholarship could cost about two Dom Leoung of Gold and half, which equals one thousand two hundred fifty ($1250) dollars. A scholarship to a "Class C" country would cost from one to one and a half Dom

Leoung of Gold, equal to from five to seven hundred fifty ($500-750) U.S dollars.

Both civil administration and police authorities, in the sub-district, known as Sangkat, and in the district, known as Khan, had to sign each individual's application to certify that the applicant had good morals and was not related to imperialism in any way. Finally, each applicant had to have a total of four signatures with stamps from the offices of these local authorities.

Reagan, Margaret and I were dreaming of having an opportunity to study in one of these countries. Every weekend four of my classmates and I always go to the Soviet Union Cultural Center to see movies, which showed the development and prosperity of that country. We all felt very excited to have an opportunity to see these documentary films. We saw big buildings and skyscrapers surrounded by beautiful parks, shops, and the metro. The underground public transportation system was very clean. We were amazed at how efficiently the Russian Government functioned. I said to myself, "Gee, the Soviet Union is like heaven".

Farmers in the Soviet Union used modern farming equipment to grow rice, corn, cotton and so on. I compared this to our farmers and said, "Gee, we grow rice by using humans, oxen and buffalos. We are so completely different, it's like heaven vs. the earth."

Every student, including myself, dreamed that after the completion of high school in Cambodia, we would receive a scholarship to study in one of these socialist countries. For us Khmer children, we thought of countries like the Soviet Union, East Germany, Bulgaria, Hungary, Poland and Czechoslovakia as heaven on earth.

Every day, during break time in school we loved to talk about our country. We exchanged ideas among five classmates: Chamroeun, Khema, Sundara, Thach Sovanna and Pheng. We would always ask the question, "Why is Cambodia so poor?" We knew the answer. It was because we, the Cambodian people, had bad leaders. Leaders like Pol Pot, Ieng Sary, Nuon Chea and Kiev Samphan who killed their own people. Leaders who were willing to sell the national interest to foreigners. Leaders who gave immunity to illegal residents because they were citizens of their foreign rulers.

One-day, the moral and discipline teacher, called my five classmates and me. We were panic stricken. We knew definitely something bad had happened. We were warned by this teacher not to talk anymore about anything related to our leaders, politics or the country.

The duty of the moral and discipline teacher is to direct the children to have good morals, to love, support and be with the communist revolution, to brain-wash these children to think that the communist revolution is the best society on earth and their own parents are not their real parents. Their biological parents just gave them birth but the communist revolution is their real parent. It takes excellent care of them in both good and bad times.

The teacher accused us of having imperialistic ideas against the PRK. He said "If I did not stop you this in time, yours ideas would grow and in the long run could harm our communist revolution." He continued, "Your job is to study, not to worry about the country. We have excellent leaders, like Comrade Seng Samrin, Chea Sim and Hun Sen to lead the country. There is nothing that you need to worry about. The high authority, known as Angkar chat tang, is concerned about this.

Finally he said, "Since you are young, I will punish you all by ordering you to clean the school's, restrooms, toilets and wash the classrooms." Before he left the classroom he said, "This is my first warning and I do not want this to happen again. I will record this incident in each of your files. This could affect you when you want to apply to be vanguard-children or communist youth. It also could affect you all when you finish high school and want to apply for a scholarship to study in our friendship countries, known as the socialist block. In short, it could affect your life forever as long as our communist state exists. The high authority, "Angkar" needs only children and youth who love the communist revolution, Angkar

Bakdevat. If you are a vanguard child or communist youth, when you apply for a scholarship, you will have priority compared to those who are not."

On that day, I came home and was so sad and felt hopeless. I said to myself, "Gee, my life has ended. I will not be able to have a higher education in the friendship countries: Soviet Union, East Germany, Bulgaria, Hungarians, Poland, Czechoslovakia and others that I considered heaven."

I kept this a secret, not telling anyone, even my super mom. I was afraid that she would be very sad if she knew something bad like this had happened to her second son.

That night, when I took a bath, I cried, feeling sorry for myself. I could not sleep very well. I dreamed of saying, "Yes, the moral teacher is completely, right." I quoted his statement, "Your job is to study not to worry about the country or anything." He was completely right. I dreamed of saying this and remembering that the eastern socialist block was a heaven on earth to me.

The following Monday my five classmates, Chamroeun, Khema, Sundara, Thack Sovanna, Pheng and I were concerned that the moral teacher would announce our faults against the communist revolution in front of everyone before students pay tribute to the flag and sing the national anthem. We did this once a week on Monday's in our school before the classes started.

The procedure was something like this: An announcement would be made if there was something wrong in the school or if any students had committed something bad or made mistakes. This was done before students started to sing the national anthem.

That Monday morning, we all looked pale with fear and concern. We looked at each other, and then turned our eyes toward the moral teacher. We all observed him in every detail.

Finally, we heard the call from the discipline teacher to call out one young boy and girl who were vanguard children from grade 5, class "C1" to prepare and raise up our national flag on the flag pole. They were to do this when they heard the national anthem music start along with the students singing.

We all were so happy. We said, "Thank God!" for helping all of us. If not, there would have been bad rumors about us in the whole school.

During the class break, we all started a discussion again but not on the same issues. I told my classmates that the moral teacher was a good man. They also thought the same too. They said that if we had done something really wrong, he would have reported it to the school authority. We believed our case was just a simple discussion and a matter of freedom of speech.

Civil war continued in the western part of Cambodia. This conflict there was between the People's Republic of Kampuchea, the new Cambodian government that had been installed by the Vietnamese Hanoi government, and the Cambodian Resistance. The Cambodian Resistance was made up of three parts. The first one was the Funcinpec, led by former King Sihanouk. The second was the Khmer National Liberation Front, led by former Prime Minister, Son San who was supported by the U.S government. The third one was the Khmer Rouge (KR) group led by the figurehead leader, Mr. Kiev Samphan who was also involved the bloodshed in Cambodia. The real power of the KR group was with Pol Pot, Nuon Chea, Ieng Sary and their local high commanders who were the leaders of killers.

There were around 300,000 (three hundred thousand) Vietnamese troops, which occupied Cambodia. They assisted the People's Republic of Kampuchea in fighting against the resistance and from the collapse of its government. These Vietnamese troop were stationed everywhere in country especially in major cities such as Phnom Penh, Kampong Som, Battambang, and Siem Reap.

At the end of 1984, the People's Republic of Kampuchea issued a policy on military service throughout the country. Each family must at least have one of their sons for call up for the army. The local authorities started registering in the family book issued by Cambodian communist government (PRK). They went from house to house. They wanted to know how many men; women, boys and girls were living in each family's house so that they could put their names on the army list for call-up.

Finally, the local authorities came to our apartment. They had my older brother Reagan on the list for the army because Reagan was considered an adult. Mom begged them to delay his time of serving in the army until he finished senior high school. They agreed with Mom since she bribed them.

Reagan and I were afraid of walking from school to home and back. We feared the local authorities, which included police, military and militia, might capture us.

The K5 Plan known as "Kor Pram" for the defense of the Cambodian--Thai border was the response of the People's Republic of Kampuchea and its Vietnamese ruler to the threat posed by the resistance forces, particularly the Khmer Rouge, to its efforts to rebuild the nation and consolidate its administration. The K5 Plan, "Kor Pram" caused thousands of Cambodians to die from hunger, landmines, bombs, and affected diseases-dengue fever, malaria, skin disease, and so on. The plan was to force the people to be as a living wall and as a defense administrative line, a living fence between the PRK and their ruler Vietnamese troops and the Cambodian resistance forces.

The plan was also to force these people to cut and clear the forest that was full of landmines and obstacles where the Cambodian resistance forces were stationed. This plan caused thousands of innocent Cambodian people to die.

The main goal of this K5 plan was to defend the country, rebuild the nation and consolidate its administration line using innocent people to die when they were attacked by the resistance forces trying to overthrown the People's Republic of Kampuchea (PRK) Government. The combined forces of the People's Army of Vietnam and the Kampuchean United Front for National Salvation declared victory over the armed forces of Democratic Kampuchea.

The Vietnamese troops cooperated with the PRK armies to conduct major military operations in the dry season after 1980. The heavily-armed Vietnamese forces were followed by the soviet military tanks: T54 and T55, Kachusa Missiles installed on military trucks that had thirty-six canon, made in the USSR, and with the air support they conducted offensive operations during the dry seasons. The resistance forces held the initiative during the rainy seasons. The resistance forces broke down into many small different groups to ambush and attack the Vietnamese and the PRK troops.

Starting from 1980 to 1984, Vietnamese troops launched a major offensive against the main Khmer Rouge base at Melai mountain, "Phnom Melai" and Anglong Veng. Vietnamese troops switched their target to refugee civilian camps near the Thai border in 1983, launching a series of massive assaults, backed by armor, heavy artillery and Kachusa missiles against refugee camps belonging to all three resistance groups.

Hundreds of civilians were injured in these attacks, and more than 90,000 refugees were forced to flee to Thailand. This Vietnamese attack also created an opportunity for Cambodian refugees to move to Thai soil and then they could escape and move to Cao-I-Dang camp. Cao-I-Dang camp was the camp for refugees who were ready to be transported to the third countries by western foreign governments. Resistance military forces, however, were largely undamaged. In the 1983-1984 dry season offensive, the Vietnamese troops again attacked the base camps of all three resistance groups. Despite stiff resistance from the guerrillas, the Vietnamese succeeded in eliminating most camps in Cambodia and drove civilian refugees into neighboring Thai territory. The resistance forces operated inside Cambodian soil.

The Vietnamese troops concentrated on consolidating their gains during the dry season, including an attempt to seal and close down all guerrilla infiltration routes into the country by using the K5 plan, forcing Cambodian laborers to clear forest, construct trenches, wire fences, and minefields along virtually the entire Thai-Cambodian border.

The Vietnamese troops, cooperating with the PRK, launched a major military offensive every dry season of the year to gain control of their administrative territorial expansion. The Dry season is the only season when they can use heavy military operations such as tank-T54 and T55 and military Kachasa missiles. In the rainy season it was kind of hard to use tanks and other support transportation because the roads are full of mud. In return the resistance forces also tried fighting by dividing in many small different groups to attack everywhere. This also made the resistance force move back and capture small provincial towns, one or two days before the Vietnamese troops and the PRK arrived. When the resistance forces controling these small towns in a short period of time, they claimed on the radio that they had control of the whole provincial area.

Even thought, the Khmer Rouge fought against the PRK, at the same time, this group continued to tyranize and kill their own people when they took over any town, district or village. This KR group was still an evil group but they were the strongest group in the resistance forces. The Funcinpec and Khmer National Liberation Front troops were not usually killing their own people. They were far better than the Khmer Rouge.

At this time, Mom was very concerned about our safety. Therefore, she made us necklaces with a symbol of Jesus Christ; each valued around five chi of gold, equal to about two hundred fifty ($250) US dollars. The plan was that if we were captured and forced to join the army, we were to give our necklace to the communist officers so that they would let us go.

Under the PRK, people were not allowed to travel from one place to another without permission. This was especially so in the

85

western part of Cambodia. The high authorities thought that people might try and escape from the country to become refugees and go to any third country or that they might surrender to the resistant Funcinpec, led by former King Sihanouk or the Khmer National Liberation Front, led by former Prime Minister, Son San who was supported by the U.S government.

All normal people who lived under the People's Republic of Kampuchea were like prisoners who live in a prison without walls. What I mean is you could not travel from one place to another but only within the administrative boundaries where you lived. The PRK government prohibited traveling. If you live in Phnom Penh, you could travel only within Phnom Penh boundaries, not outside of the boundaries of the city. If you did, you would be caught and sent to prison.

My Wedding Ceremony. L-R: Uncle Sokhak, Aunt Sar, My lovely wife Romona, Me, My Mom and My Sister Margaret

Me and My Mom

My brother Reagan and My Mom

The People's Republic of Kampuchea (PRK) 1984-1985
My Life in Another Communist Regime (PRK)

In early 1984 my older brother Reagan was a senior in high school. He applied for a higher education scholarship to study in one of the Friendship Socialist Countries under the sponsorship of our Uncle Sokhak. Uncle Sokhak was a pharmacist and the Chief Bureau Technique of the Second Kampuchean Pharmaceutical Factory of the Ministry of Public Health. He was also a member of the lowest civil service office of the communist, known as "Snol".

Reagan was granted a scholarship to study in the Socialist Republic of Vietnam (SRV). He decided not to go for higher education in Vietnam because the scholarship that was granted by the government was a very poor one, not enough to pay for daily living expenses.

Fortunately, we had our father's friend Ho Van who had survived from the Khmer Rouge regime. He worked for the Department of Education in the Ministry of Education. In 1985, my mom asked him to sponsor Reagan to study in one of the friendship socialist countries. He agreed and signed the educational application form. He listed Reagan as his nephew. He advised Reagan not to try to escape to any capitalist country while he was studying. If Reagan did, "Uncle" Ho Van would be held responsible. He might be demoted or dismissed from his position or be sent to prison. Later, he was assigned by the PRK Ministry of Education to be the Cambodian Educational and Cultural Representative first in former USSR and later East Germany. His job there was to assist Cambodian students with whatever they needed while they were studying abroad.

During this time, Reagan, his schoolfellows and all senior high school students who studied in Phnom Penh city were given medical check-ups by a group of Russian Medical Doctors to find out who had good mental and physical health, good vision and excellent study records. This was to choose the young men to learn to fly the military air fighter MIC 21 and civil airplanes.

Reagan's friend, Sophoan, passed his medical test. He was sponsored by his father who was a communist government public employee working for the Railway Station Department under the Ministry of Public Work. Sophoan was granted a scholarship to study in the Union of Soviet Socialist Republics (USSR) to be a civil pilot.

A couple of months later, with the help of my father's friend, Reagan was also granted a scholarship by the PRK educational department under the ministry of education to study in the former USSR. He was so excited and very happy. Before their departure, all of the Cambodian students had to pass other medical tests. Reagan was not worried about this since he had gone through all of his medical tests at the Cambodia-Soviet Friendship Hospital and the result had come out great.

Aeroflot, the Russian Airline, would transport all of these students. The whole airplane was devoted to these students. There weren't any other passengers. They normally stopped over in Bombay, India or sometime in Dubai, the United Arab Emirates in transit. Finally they arrived in Moscow. For those students who would study in Russia, they were all set. They were welcomed by the Russian Educational University Representative to take them to their dormitory. The next day, they had to have another medical exam then they started studying the Russian language for one year before they started studying their subject area. This procedure was the same for the Cambodia students who studied elsewhere.

For those students who would study in East Germany, Hungaria, Bulgaria, Czechoslovakia and Poland they continued the trip to their destination. But don't forget, those students who had an opportunity to study in any of these five communist countries were considered to be the luckiest persons because these countries provided not only the highest national living standard but also a quality education. I mean that not only was enough food provided but also it was of good quality, not like other countries, e.g. Vietnam (SRV) where the food quality was poor and limited in amount, not enough for daily needs.

The People's Republic of Kampuchea (PRK) signed an educational agreement with these friendship socialist countries to allow Cambodian students to study there. In return, the Government provided rubber and raw material to them. For Bachelor's, Master's and the Ph.D. degree, the (PRK) provided five tons, six tons, or seven tons of rubber and raw material respectively in exchange for higher education for its students. One ton is equal to one thousand kilograms. These conditions created a hard burden for the PRK.

Reagan still wanted to go to a western country. He had a classmate known as "Mo" who had a connection to a ship captain who transported cargo from other countries to Cambodia and vice versa. The ship captain and his group charged each person who wanted to escape one domloeung of gold, which equals about four hundred and fifty ($450.00) U.S dollars.

One morning Reagan got up around 1:00 A.M to travel in a cargo truck to Sihanouk Ville, Kampong Som seaport. He was advised to disguise himself as a truck cargo porter. Around 5:30 A.M he and all of the other people arrived in Kampong Som. With the arrangement of the ship captain and his group, Reagan and the other people were allowed to enter the seaport secretly.

They all were waiting for the signal from the ship captain's men to be on board in the bottom of the ship. They all would hide in the cargo box that was supposed to transport material to different foreign countries. They normally dropped these boat people at sea in international waters. Then it was up to them to survive. Sometimes, the coast guard of any country helped them. Sometimes they were robbed and killed by the international pirates or the coast guards. Mostly coast guards of the Thai Kingdom killed these boat people instead of helping them.

Unfortunately, the ship did not have an order to leave the seaport for their destination. Around 8:00 A.M the ship was checked and surrounded by the military, the police, and custom officers. They found the people, which included men, women, boys and girls. They arrested them and sent them to jail. Some even were shot to death and killed for trying to escape from the military and police.

Fortunately, with the assistant of his friend "Mo" and the ship captain's men, Reagan was not hiding in the cargo box. Since he was disguised as a sea cargo porter, he was able to escape the local authorities. After the incident had happened, Reagan managed to escape. He stayed there for a day and at night and then made it back to Phnom Penh. By that time Reagan had lost three hundred U.S dollars. He had been given a discounted price from the original price of four hundred and fifty because he knew the ship captain's relative, his friend "Mo".

Mom could not sleep well at night because she was concerned about her Son safety. Mom always prayed day and night for him. Two days later, Reagan managed to come back home safety. Reagan was the one that Mom worried about the most. Since he was the oldest among us, Mom wanted him to go to a western country then later if everything went well; he would be the main source to help our family in return.

After arriving home for a couple of weeks, he finally, made a secret trip to the Thai border again. He arrived there safely. He stayed in the Nang Chan and Nang Sameth refugee camp along the Thai-Cambodia border. These two camps were located in Cambodian territory. He tried to go to Cao-E-Dang camp, which was located in the Thai territory but it was impossible.

The Thai army guarded all the roads and checkpoints so he could not cross the border into Cao-E-Dang camp. The only way one could have an opportunity and possibility to go to a western country was to be in the Cao-E-Dang camp. This camp had many charities, Christian, international, Red Cross, and other non-governmental organizations who worked there. If you had money, you could hide and the human smugglers who had a strong connection to the Thai military would take you there but it was very risky. One was often cheated, robbed, and sometimes arrested or killed. Sometimes, it was a trap of the smugglers and the soldiers they knew. A human life during this period (the evil regime-Khmer Rouge, the PRK during the civil and ideological war between the communist and capitalist) was not worth as much as a cat or dog in a western country. There most cats and dogs have enough food to eat with good health care.

If one wanted to escape, one had to be willing to take great, life or death, risks. The Thai army and the Khmer Rouge soldiers were very similar. They killed people like chickens and ducks. Perhaps the Thais were a bit better. Even so they opened fire and killed those innocent people who tried to enter their territory.

During this time, it seemed like the PRK authorities allowed markets and other mini private businesses back on a very small scale under the strict control from the communist government.

Margaret and I were in the 6th grade of Bak Touk Junior High School. After school, I had to help Mom by taking clothes and materials to the tailor shops. Mom would do the account reconciliation the following day, based on my records. As a part of that, I helped Mom in selling clothes at the stand in Ouressey Market.

Every day, I had to get up very early, carry clothes and materials on my old bicycle to Mom's stand in Ouressey market before going to school. In the afternoon before the market was closed, I helped Mom pack the material and put it into the locker on Mom's stand. The most important and valuable clothes and materials I would carry back home by bicycle.

Mom's business did not go well because of a very low demand and too many suppliers. The country economy was really bad. Most normal people could not afford to buy anything. We continued to have daily food problem. We never had enough food to eat, not only in the Khmer Rouge but also in the PRK regime. But indeed, in PRK regime is much better than the KR regime.

Every time Margaret and I were sick, the magic medicine that could cure our illness was Chinese noodle soup with beef, meatball, bean sprouts and salad. Normally, after having this delicious vitamin soup, we were well again. Mostly Reagan's and my sickness was caused by the lack of food to eat and vitamins in our bodies. That is why we all, Margaret, Reagan and I stopped growing.

Every year in the dry season, especially in the 1984-1985 dry season offensive, the Vietnamese attacked base camps of all three resistance groups. Civil war continued without end. Every day there were lots of people killed and injured.

Because of international pressure, the Vietnamese were planning to withdraw part of their troops from Cambodia.

Every day, after school and Mom's work, our family, Mom, Margaret and I were always sad and worried about our future. At this time, my family had lots of problems. The major problem was our lack of daily food, the second problem was Mom's poor business and the third one was the problem that we were not allowed to stay in our apartment, Bloc Seng Thai.

Mom received an order that we must leave our apartment within 30 days. We were not going to receive any compensation from the communist authorities. If we didn't leave, we were warned that the whole family would be arrested and sent to jail.

At this time, Mom was worried too death. Not only about our daily life but where we could stay and how were we to survive. She also worried about Reagan's safety. If he could not get to Cao-E-Dang camp in Thailand, he needed to get back to Phnom Penh by the third week of August 1985 so that he could go to study in the Soviet Union.

Mom and I cried every night and prayed that the Lord might help us. I also thought that when I grew up, I would take revenge on those who had tyrannized my family and made us suffer so much during this time.

These ideas for revenge were always on my mind. When I went to school, to help Mom's business in Ouressey market or anywhere I thought, "When I complete my high school education, I will apply for a scholarship to study in the Soviet Union to be a military air fighter. Then when I finish my study there, I would come back to Cambodia to fly air fighters. When I had a mission to fly to bomb the Khmer Rouge, I would take that opportunity to take my Mom and sister on the plane with me to bomb and open fire on all the communist apartment buildings that belonged to those who had tyrannized and made my family suffer. Then I would fly to Thailand or Singapore.

Another plan that I considered was that when I was in the pilot military training school in the Soviet Union and when there was a test flight, I could escape with a MIC 21 and fly it to a country nearby or to Finland. After thinking more about this, I realized it was not a good idea because Mom and my sister would still be living in Cambodia and they would be arrested and spend a lifetime in jail. I concluded that I could not do this. I could not just want to have freedom for myself in a western country and cause my family to be in danger.

I sometimes wanted to commit a suicide or to kill other people who that made my family suffer. But on the other hand, I thought it would be worse if I did so because my family would suffer because of my actions.

I understand how people can kill others when they feel great injustice, suffering, pain and all the tragedy that they have. In those days I always asked myself why my live, my family's and all other

Cambodian's lives were suffering so greatly, not only from hunger and starvation but also we were tyrannized. These were things I thought people in the western world knew nothing about and had never experienced.

We Cambodian people lived through this hardship. We saw with our own eyes that the military and the police of the Khmer Rouge and the PRK killed innocence people as if they were killing wild animals. The military and the police were established to safeguard the people and the country but instead they used their authority to kill people who opposed their ideas.

That is why, most people like me who have gone through the Khmer Rouge and the PRK regimes, hate the military and the police so much because we see them as ignorant instruments that the evil communist government used to kill their own people. I always asked myself, how could the police and military have the heart to kill their own people when they get the evil order from their masters to do so???

Why they don't think and react back to their evil masters??? Why are the military and the police so ignorant??? Why do they do what they have been told to do so without any consideration and consciousness?

Indeed there was answer, they fear about their family as well if they do not implement and respect the order from their communist master.

In the Khmer Rouge and PRK, every time, we common people saw the police and the military, we always though that we met evil people who were going to take our lives or to harm us or put us in danger. That is why we hate these police and military. Our mindset of fear of the military and the police remains until now.

Finally, Reagan came back home in time to take up the scholarship. Since he had been out of Phnom Penh for a long time, we all were worried that the Department of Education might omit his name from the scholarship list. Indeed, he had a problem because of his absence. They accused him of being a national traitor by escaping from the country to the western world.

Now, it was our super Mom's jobs again to bride the Department of Education officers. She gave them some money and claimed that Reagan had gone to Kampot province because my father's grandma who lived there was really sick and he had to be there to take good care of her. With the approval letter issued by the local authority, the charges were dropped against Reagan and he was allowed to go to study in the Soviet Union.

After the help, Reagan finally made his way to the Soviet Union. We thought he was the luckiest in the family. He had spent most of the money from Mom's personal property. If not, our family- Mom, Margaret and I could have used that gold to exchange for food for our daily lives and we could have enough food to eat. We thought he was now going to be in heaven for the next five years. What I mean was that we believed that Reagan was going to be in a good country that had a high living standard and have a much better life than ours would be in Cambodia. What he needs to worry about was only his study. If he fails the course there, he would be sent back home and be imprisoned. He was not going to suffer a lot like my sister, Margaret and I were.

During this time, I still continued my English study at the hiding place. There were only a few students. I did not attend school regularly because Mom could not afford to pay for my English school fee. I told my English teacher that Mom could not afford for me to be in school regularly and she said it was ok not to pay once in a while but not always because she needed to survive too. I was the only one that Mom allowed to study. Margaret did not have an opportunity to study English because Mom didn't have enough money for both of us.

The communist officers looked down on our family. Every time, they saw my sister, Margaret and I walking from school or Mom's business, they looked at us in a bad manner from head to toe and from toe to head showing hatred and sometimes, they said, "Tell your Mom to move out from this apartment within 30 days, if not, we will bring the military and the police to arrest your whole family and send you to jail." They continued, "You are the simple people. Angkar does not allow you to live here. This place is only for the communist senior cadre."

When they did that to us, it felt like they were going to take their knife and kill us. I asked myself why these people hate us so much. Every time, they saw Mom walking across the apartment grounds, they did the same. They stopped her and threatened her. Mom had to give them some personal valuables, like gold. If she did give it to them, they would stop for a while but two or three months later, they acted like this again.

Every time they stopped Mom she always cried with tears dropping down from her eyes and she replied, "Where do you want me to move, comrade woman? I need a place to stay like you do. Beside that I have my children, nephew and niece to feed. What you want me to do, now??? Please let my family and me survive! We survived through out the most evil Khmer Rouge. I definitely knew that the PRK Angkar want me and my children to survive too so that they can help Angkar to rebuild our country. Please do not hurt my children. You can hurt me but not them, please. I need them to see the world that Angkar wants them to see. They are the white paper that Angkar needs. They know nothing about the imperialist and capitalism. They are genuine and pure that our Angkar needs as talent to reconstruct our country.

Seeing this situation with Mom crying and sometimes collapsing, one of the communist senior officials who lived there told them to leave and stop their action. This man had pity on my Mom and our family.

Now, everywhere in Phnom Penh including school, government institutions and everywhere else across the country, they forced people to join the army to fight the Khmer Rouge. According to the

PRK rule and regulation, each family had to have at least one family member to join the army.

In Phnom Penh during this tension filled year, while walking from school or one place to another place in public, the military in civil uniforms grabbed people when they passed by and threw them into a military truck and drove away.

Sometimes, if people escaped and ran away, the communist military and the police used their evil tricks to shoot at them or they shouted loud that they were thieves so that they could seek to catch them.

During the PRK regime, I hardly saw any thieves because if you stole something and were caught by the communist, sometimes they would just kill you and say you were part of the Khmer Rouge. There was no organization to investigate this. If you were gone there was no one to help you.

In the communist PRK, the crime rate was nearly zero. The city was very safe because the government controlled everything; especially how many people were in each family. If there was a new comer from another area to visit your family, you had to report to the local authority and that person must have a letter of travel approval from their original local authority. One could not walk and travel in and around the city at night. The city had a curfew from 9:30PM to 6:30AM.

Everywhere in the city there were checkpoints, especially on the main road that one had to travel in order to come into the city. Each checkpoint normally had five to seven military men with AK-47 rifles, grenades and a full pack of arms and ammunition on each of them.

If they stopped you, you must stop. There was a no chase policy. If you did not stop, they automatically opened fire to kill you. Then if you were killed, they just said, you were the Khmer Rouge.

Through out Cambodia, there were around two or three hundred thousand Vietnamese troops deployed in the PRK regime. In Phnom Penh, every night you saw the Vietnamese troops were on patrol within the delegate zone. In a part of that zone, the PKR troops were on patrol as well.

If someone knew the Vietnamese troops, its local commander or one of their experts, you had a strong connection. The PRK communist respected you because you knew their big master. You can do whatever you wanted to do. You can take any property and claim it is yours or you can do anything except kill people. The PRK communist did not bother you or gave you any kind of trouble.

All of the PRK senior ministers and its officials were afraid of the Vietnamese experts, troops and commanders because they were the rulers of the PRK communist regime.

At this time, I was concerned about my safety. I was afraid that I might be caught and forced to join the army. For my family, now, I was the only one that the PRK would pick to join the army because my brother Reagan had gone to the Soviet Union. Based on the PRK rule, I would be his replacement.

Now, in schools across the nation, all students who were in junior and senior high school have to learn military training tactics. I learned not only how to use an AK-47 and the M16 that the communist said "it was used by the U.S imperialist and their puppets" but also how to move slowly by drawing the body along the ground, crawling. I also learned how to install, to take it off and reinstall AK-47 and M16 rifle again. We had to study these topics every year until we finished high school.

Under the PRK, the educational system was divided into three parts. First, there was primary school, which started from Class 1 to class 4. One had to pass a primary school national examination before you could enter to Junior High School or the PRK term known as Level One High School, which started from class 5 to class 7. It was the same thing, you had to pass your junior high school national examination before you could be accepted to be in Senior High School or known as Level Two High School, which started from class 8 to class 10. In senior high school, you were required to study Russian and Vietnamese languages. So, you had an opportunity to study foreign languages: Russian and Vietnamese for three years.

Therefore, one could complete high school education in only 10 years under the People's Republic of Kampuchea (PRK) educational schooling system.

The People's Republic of Kampuchea (PRK) 1985-1986
My Life in Another Communist PRK regime

At this time our family consisted of only the three of us: our super mom, sister Margaret and me. We were living in Phnom Penh. Reagan was in Moscow, the capital of the Union of Soviet Socialist Republics, for his higher education. He and his teammates of twenty-two Cambodian students were allowed to stay in Moscow only two weeks for their medical check ups. Then, they were sent to the Ukraine to study the Russian language for a whole year before they could begin to study their subject areas.

Margaret and I were in high school. My good teacher advised me that I should apply to join the Communist Youth Alliance (CYA) so that when I completed high school, I would have a chance to compete for a scholarship to study in the friendship socialist countries.

My friends, Porsreang, Sundara, Pheng, Sovanna, Chamroeun, Khema and I went regularly to school every Thursday to clean up the school (restrooms and toilets), grow plants, and serve as student security guards at night and during the day after class. We were assigned to guard the school once a week at night and three times a week during the day. We were working hard to become Communist Youth Alliance members. We completed a youth application form, which included all of our personal data with the name of our sponsor. The form had to be certified by both local authorities, civil and police, to state level that we were good citizens. If any family member had been related to any organization considered imperial or feudal, the application would be denied. We had written clearly that our family's background was simple, good, clean and NOT RELATED in any way with IMPERIALISM or FEUDALISM.

We submitted our applications to the Communist Youth Alliance and Discipline Council Committee for approval so that we could become Youth Alliance (CYA) members. We believed this would help us when we graduated from high school, if we wanted to apply for a scholarship to study in any friendship socialist country or work in the government of the People's Republic of Kampuchea (PRK).

The educational governmental selection committee gave priority ranking to students whose sponsors were (a) senior communist officials at the intermediate, medium, or low level, (b) Communist Youth Alliance members, and finally to those students with (c) simple citizen sponsors.

My close friend Porsreang, a Chinese-Khmer, whose parents had emigrated from China a very long time ago and settled in Cambodia as permanent residents, had helped me a lot. Every day, at break time in school, he always paid for me for everything, even breakfast. What I mean is, if he had breakfast, he treated me to breakfast too. He was kind and a good-hearted friend. His family owned a small business for repairing motorboats, motorcycles and vehicles. His family was categorized as part of the 351 groups, a Chinese-Khmer ethnic group in the PRK regime.

More than six months after we submitted our Youth application forms, we began to check with the Communist Youth Alliance and the Discipline Council Committee (CYA & DCC). Each time we were informed that our applications were under consideration and that a background investigation of each individual was underway. The head of CYA & DCC called each of us, one at a time up to his office. He said the same thing each time; that there was nothing to worry about concerning the application, that we should concentrate on our work and study hard with good moral behavior for the revolution. He said, "During these years the CYA & DCC observes your performance. You have to prove your ability with excellent morals for our revolution as a communist. You must know that the CYA & DCC selects only students who have good and clean backgrounds. The investigation may take years. Time will tell. The revolution does not need you if you do not meet the requirements, even you are a genius in school."

My friends and I felt that we might be cheated by the Communist Youth Alliance and the Discipline Council Committee (CYA & DCC). Maybe they just wanted to use us to help in doing the schoolwork which included cleaning and being security guards. We also did field trips to help the peasants who lived near Phnom Penh. We went to help harvest their rice crops. Groups from my school with around 500 students or more went with the guidance from their teachers and CYA & DCC. We had to arrange for our own transportation, usually bicycle, to the destinations.

We were confident that our friend, Porsreang, would not be accepted by the Communist Youth Alliance and Discipline Council Committee (CYA & DCC) because his family was classified as being part of the 351 groups. This was a crucial point at that time when the Beijing government fully supported the Khmer Rouge's attempt to overthrow the People's Republic of Kampuchea (PRK)'s regime. The Beijing government was also the enemy of PRK's ruler, the Hanoi government.

There were lots of advantages to being a member of the Communist Youth Alliance (CYA). It was said that it would help us overcome hardships. It was clear that the communist government valued this status. Therefore, we realized that we needed to be a member of CYA if we wanted to have a good life in the future. Membership was compared to a white paper with a pure heart. It was proof that the communist government had developed you from childhood, starting from primary school, as a Vanguard child, then on up the ladder to finally when one in high school, becoming a CYA member.

If you were a Communist Youth Alliance member when you got a job with the PRK government, first you would be a simple public official with recognition. When you were promoted, you received the first title of "Snol", which was the first level of a communist member's rank. The second was "Pakka Chun", a party member. The third, "Kama Pibal", a Senior Official of the communist party. With "Kama Pibal", Senior Official rank and "Pakka Chun", party member rank, you were entitled to have governmental privileges, which included such things as a vehicle with a driver. A "Sivphov Kama Pibal", known as book of Kama Pibal allowed you to get free food, drinks, clothes, study materials, commodities, etc. from the government business center.

Most of our neighbors were senior government official. They all had "Sivphov Kama Pibal", known as book of Kama Pibal. This was the privilege that they had over normal people.

I always dreamed that one day, when I grew up, I would become the Cambodian Top Leader. Most of my uncles were educated persons with degrees in economics, pharmacy, political science, etc. My dream was that then, I would assign all my relatives to hold ministerial positions in my government, especially in the military, police, finance and foreign affairs. I would lead Cambodia differently from all former regimes. Then, I would also have the ability to take revenge and bring all the former leaders of the killers to justice.

Mom always told me that revenge is based on ignorance. With revenge, the bloodshed and the killing would never end. Mom said we had to forgive and to forget. I asked her, "How can you forgive those who killed and tyrannized our family? The Khmer Rouge regime's top leaders like Pol Pot, Ieng Sary, Nuon Chea, Ta Mok, Khiev Samphan and others senior military commanders who gave the orders to their local authorities to kill their own innocent people?"

I said we had to bring them all to justice, especially their local henchmen.

If I were the leader, my main focus would be to make Cambodia and her people prosperous and happy. First, we would develop public transportation--roads and highways that could link the entire country together for economic facilitation and development. Second, electricity would be provided to everyone through out the country and third, clean and pure drinking water with an irrigation network throughout the nation. In addition, we would develop an educational system and businesses in rural areas so they could make progress as in the cities. Therefore, jobs would be created and there would be an economic boom.

Every day, I was eager to learn about the top key leaders of the People's Republic of Kampuchea, its Revolutionary Party Central Committee and Politburo Members which included Heng Samrin, Hun Sen, Chea Sim, Chea Soth, Chan Si, Chan Seng, Chan Phinh, Koy Buntha, Say Chhum, Say Bouthang, Bou Thang, Keo Chenda, Tea Banh and also the Khmer Rouge leaders, including Pol Pot, Ieng Sary, Nuon Chea, Khiev Samphan, Son Sen and Ta Mok.

First, I tried to get all sizes of photos of these top leaders from where ever I could find them- in books, PRK banner advertisement and at the national library, near Wat Phnom. I started to study these people from all angles. Their faces, eyes, eyes brows, ears, noses and mouths. Then, I tried to get big photos with large images to see and identify a person, and learn why this person, Ieng Sary or Pol Pot or Nuon Chea for example was so cruel??? The more I looked at Ieng Sary, Pol Pot and Nuon Chea's image, the more I learned that they was a henchman and a killer.

The communist leaders was sweet talk but their real actions was completely different-cruel, barbarous and inhumanity.

I wanted to know who these people were. Where did they come from? How did they become the top leaders in the government? Who assisted them? I definitely knew that the Hanoi government was the one who promoted them. What is their personality like? I wanted to meet them personally and talk to them so that I could collect information and learn to evaluate who was the good-hearted leader with national interest and who was the killer of their own people.

I love to talk to old people. I asked them to compare the Sangkum Reas Niyum Regime, led by King Sihanouk, Khmer Republic, led by Marshall Lon Nol, the Democratic of Kampuchea known as Khmer Rouge regime, led by leaders of Killer Pol Pot, Ieng Sary, Nuon Chea, Son Sen, Ta Mok and Khiev Samphan and the People's Republic of Kampuchea, led by President Heng Samrin.

Most of the old people I talked with told me that they loved Sangkum Reas Niyum Regime that was led by King Sihanouk. They told me that most people including city people as well as farmers and peasants who lived in the countryside had a good standard of living then. The country was at peace. Our people had high morals, dignity and were helpful to one another. But what they didn't like was when King Sihanouk allowed the communist of Vietnam, the Viet Cong, and the Hanoi regime to use Cambodian territory to fight against South Vietnam that was supported by the U.S Government.

For Cambodian people who were educated, they said, they liked the Khmer Republic regime because the country was so powerful, both economically and militarily. We stood and built our borders with our neighboring countries. What they didn't like about this period was that the country was at civil war and the Government was corrupt.

I asked lots of people about President Heng Samrin of the People's Republic of Kampuchea and Chea Sim who was his Minister of Interior. They told me that Chea Sim and Heng Samrin used to be King Sihanouk's loyalist during their communist movement against the Lon Nol regime. In my personal opinion, these two leaders seem to be simple but there might be a situation that can force them both to do something that the people did not expect.

All people preferred to talk about Sangkum Reas Niyum Regime that was led by King Sihanouk, the Khmer Republic regime and the Khmer Rouge, but not the PRK. Some people told me, "do not talk about politics if you do not want to go jail." They were scared of people. They did not know who could be trusted. People might work as secret agents for the PRK. Who's known??? To avoid problems, just don't talk about politics.

By talking to old people and having the opportunity to meet some King Sihanoukist who was now working for the PRK, I found out that most Sihanoukist loyalist supporters were mostly good simple men.

Heng Samrin was born in 1934 in Prey Veng province. He was little known until his installation as the head of PRK by the Vietnamese in whose name the Vietnamese used to justify their invasion of Cambodia in 02 December 1978. Between 1976-1978, Heng Samrin served as political commissar and commander of Democratic Kampuchea's fourth division stationed in the eastern zone. In May 1978, he was involved in a failed rebellion against Pol Pot's leadership and fled to Vietnam to escape a political purge.

Heng Samrin entered Cambodia with the Vietnamese invading forces and was appointed the president of the State Council and Secretary General of the People's Revolutionary Party of Kampuchea and served in that capacity until 1989.

In May 1981, Hun Sen became a member of the Politburo of the Kampuchean People's Revolutionary Party Central Committee, and Deputy Chairman of the PRK Council of Ministers. He was then third in rank on the Politburo. On January 14, 1985, following the sudden death of Chan Si on December 31, 1984, Hun Sen was unanimously elected Chairman of the People's Republic of Kampuchea Council of Ministers by the National Assembly.

I talked to my barber regularly. He seemed to know all about Hun Sen. He told me that Hun Sen left home, Kampong Cham province, when he was thirteen to study in a pagoda, in Phnom Penh. Then at the age of fourteen he left the city and joined the Khmer communist movement, which was supported by the Vietcong of North Vietnam. His favorite leader was Ieng Sary. Hun Sen met Ieng Sary in Kampong Cham rural area during Ieng Sary's trip to check and follow up on the movement's progress in the liberation zones. During the meeting, he called Ieng Sary, comrade "Bon." When you call someone "BON", you respect, give favor or are showing great politeness to that person.

He continued to tell me that Hun Sen was a man who dared to do everything even sabotage, ambush, plot against Marshal Lon Nol Government. This might involve people's life by the order of the high communist movement. It seems to me that his action was forced by the situation to allow him to do so. When he got an order from a person who has high authority in the organization, he and his group implemented it by armbushing, attacking and opening fire on government military station and property or even on the people. This act is known as an act of sabotage. Then, he and his group would escape to the deep forest.

I learned that Mr. Hun Sen was moving ahead of his comrades in arms. This was based on two things. First, he had a strong and close relationship of support from the Vietnamese, Vietcong. Second, he was smart in a military leadership and had his own army brigade.

In school, I enjoyed learning about history and moral discipline. I learned about each of the presidents of the former USSR: Yury Andropov's, Leonid Ilyich Brezhnev, Konstontin Chernenko and Mikhail Govbachev. Their childhood, education, background, communist activities and how they became the top Russian leader. For example over the course of Yury Andropove's 15 month tenure (1982-84) as general secretary of the Communist Party, Gorbachev became one of the Politburo's most highly active and visible members; and, after he died and Konstantin Chernenko became general secretary in February 1984, Gorbachev became a likely successor to the latter. Chernenko died on March 10, 1985, and the following day the Politburo elected Gorbachev general secretary of the Communist Party of the Soviet Union. Upon his accession, he was still the youngest member of the Politburo.

The moral discipline class was the one that I did not understand and had lots of questions. For example my teacher said, "We were very lucky to have opportunities to live in a socialist country. We did not have social classes. Everyone was equal. Our military and police were the instruments to safeguard the country and to protect our people from harm and danger." But in every day life I saw it completely different from the theories that I learned in school. I saw just the opposite. No student was allowed to ask questions, or have comments. What the teacher said was right. It was our job to listen and put it in our hearts. The teacher said we were socialist at present, and this was a transition to communism. When we reached that, our people would have all their basic needs met. One can work less but their needs and demands would be fulfilled because the country and her people would be prosperous under communism.

Through my observation I was smart enough to figure out that even my teacher was just a mouthpiece for the higher organization. They told him what to say; he himself could not express his own opinion. Those were the orders that people in the whole country had to follow. One could ask thousands and thousands of people but the answer would be the same thing because they were afraid to talk. If you dared to talk or express your opinion, you disappeared quickly.

Like Mom said, to survive in any environment, we had to use the experience that we had learned during the Khmer Rouge regime. That was "rean dam doeum kor"-- be silent. We compared this to "Kor tree" where one had to pretend that s/he did not hear anything and no one spoke openly about anything. Like the saying during the Khmer Rouge time, if the authority did not ask you, you did not need to answer, just keep what you know in secret.

I was an outgoing kid. I liked talking a lot. I complained about this and that. When I saw something was wrong or not quite right, I had to talk about it. I could not hold my thoughts to myself. Every day, I saw injustice happen. Mom told me that to learn to survive, I had keep quiet or at least talk less. Listen more and think before you talk was her advice. She warned, " Review it over and over to make sure that if you thought comes out how it could affect or impact the other people".

In my Bak Touk School, there were two children of Nhoun Nhel, the governor of Phnom Penh. Two daughters of Vietnamese experts working in Cambodia, the son of the Minister of Information and Culture, the son of the Minister of Interior and sons and daughters of other high profile government officials.

My friends: Porsreang, Sundara, Pheng, Sovanna, Chamroeun, Khema and I regularly talked to each one of them who were in different classes. School had classified students into different classes. One class contained between 40-50 students. Each class was named and counted from "A" to "Z". We were in class "C".

We exchanged views about issues in our country and the situation both economically and politically. After the discussion, we realized that all of these high profile government children supported the PRK. Therefore, we were different in ideology and philosophy. We were warned that if we discussed any issue related to the PRK and politics, the policemen would catch us. In every school and university throughout the country, there were students who worked under covered for the secret police of the ministry of interior and ministry of national defense. Students who worked under cover for the government normally had small short guns known as "Praha" which were made in Czechoslovakia.

One day Porsreang asked me to have Chinese noodle soup with him after school. He told me that he would pay for me. We both went to a local Chinese noodle soup cart, which was set up on the sidewalk of the Boulevard, Charle Degaul in front of the French architecture building, near our school. This cart moved from one place to another. The cart was open on all four sides. It was setting up in an open air.

The noodle seller is the cook and normally he had one assistant who acted as waiter or waitress. The assistant stood on one side and serviced the clients who sat on those three sides remaining in the open air. They moved around town from one place to another. The assistant bangs the two small pieces of bamboo on each other making noise like, "Tlok tok tok; Tlok tok tok; Tlok tok tok". People hear this sound within three to four hundred meters. This sound indicates that the noodle soup cart is coming so people come out and buy.

While there, we saw three military police officers in the distance. We both were scared of them. I told Porsreang to walk out and go to another place. Porsreang said the police might think that we were trying to escape from them and they might arrest us without any reason.

I told Porsreang that they might arrest us if they got angry. We knew we were not going to make direct eye contact. By accident, when I grabbed a chair and looked up, my eyes made contact with them. They shouted at my friend and me and said, "Down with these two 351 group members! Do you want to die? Is that why you both looked at me in the eyes directly?" We just said nothing back.

Most military and police in Cambodia, didn't want you to have direct eye contact with them. They feel intimidated and they thought you might fight back. If you did make eye contact, they might threaten you or say something worse like, "Do you want to die?"

We knew that they were so frustrated waiting for their noodle soup to be done. Finally, it was done and the assistant brought each one of them with a big bowl of special hot noodle soup. When you ordered a "special", the soup contained more meat, which included beef, pork, bone as well as a lot of meatballs. These military police were not patient. They used their power to threaten the seller and his assistant. They shouted to the seller and his assistant and called them members of the 351 groups and said that was the reason they did things very badly and very slowly. They said, "I will not pay for it." The more they shouted, the more nervous the assistant got. Suddenly, the hot soup was spilled on one of them. Then they got really mad. One of them took out his pistol from his waist and shot the girl in the leg.

We were both stunned and laid down on the ground. We heard three bullets, "Panh, panh, and panh." Two bullets missed. And the other one went into her thigh in her leg. Because we were stunned, we couldn't move and said nothing. A couple of minutes later we were able to shout "Oh, my God" "Oh, my God" "Oh, my God". Blood were spewing everywhere. One of them said, "Damn, damn, damn." if you continued to shout I would have shot you both. There is no God who can help you and this girl. Then they just left without paying the bill and left the victim there.

Porsreang and I asked for help. Finally, the local district police arrived on their bicycles and took a report on what was happened. We knew that there was nothing that they could do about it. If it's gone it's gone. Unless, you have your family working in the government as "Kama Pibal", Senior Official rank, party member "pak kor chhun" or "snol" who can help you to bring this military police to justice.

On that sad day, we both packed the noodle soup home and said good-bye to each other. We walked home with a feeling of heavy-hearted pity for the victim who was shot just like it was a small thing. I asked my self again and again, "How can people do this? How can people do this? How can people do this?!"

I saw many things that the military police did which caused trouble and problems. They shot people like they were wild animals. That is when my anger toward the military and the police began. I actually grew to hate them and to believe that most of them were killers.

The People's Republic of Kampuchea (PRK) 1986-1987
My Life in Another Communist PRK regime

Time had gone so fast. After more than eight months since Reagan left Phnom Penh for Moscow, our family was extremely excited to receive a letter with photos from him in the USSR.

In his letter, Reagan described his daily life--study, food and allowance. He had studied the Russian language for more than seven months up to one year. During the summer, he and his group worked on a Russian apple and grape farm to pick apples and grapes. He said that he and his group received a monthly allowance of 80 (Eighty) Ruble in Russian currency from the Russian Educational Institution to spend for their daily living: food, clothes and other expenses.

Reagan said that 80 (Eighty) Ruble per month was just enough for only food. He needed to work in a Russian farm or factory in the summer and save the money earned in order to survive during his study there. Reagan had enclosed three photos, which were taken at Ukraine University. I saw that the landscape was beautiful and the University was clean.

Cambodian students from families who were well off, visited Cambodia during the summer and returned to the USSR before the school started in September. They had to buy their own air ticket. The government did not sponsor for their visit. They took back to Russia all kind of clothes--jeans, Levis and jackets to trade there. That kind of business was great. Most Cambodian students conducted business by bringing lots of clothes to trade there in order to survive during their student days.

Reagan told us that the Union of Soviet Socialist Republics (USSR) is a socialist country but their people have enough food to eat. The Soviet Union is a progressive country in all fields, economic, industrial, farming, agriculture, military and technology. He also praised the Russian leaders.

Cambodia, Vietnam and Laos used only mechanical products from the USSR, including bicycles, motorcycles, cars, trucks; mostly everything. Cambodia exchanged our local raw rubber materials for these Russian products.

Cambodia, as a socialist country, was completely different from other socialist countries. Our people were very poor. We did not have enough to eat. The country did not produce any local manufactured goods. Our roads and means of transportations were primitive. We could not even travel throughout the nation by road. In every category, we seemed to be at the bottom of anyone's list of nations.

Reagan encouraged me to do my best in studies so that I would have an opportunity to study abroad, in a socialist friendship country. That way I could avoid being forced into the army to fight against the Khmer Rouge.

There were three opportunities for scholarships. One was when a student completed his/her sophomore year in high school. If you applied for a governmental scholarship at that time and it was granted, you would be able to have three years of study abroad and it was expected that you would return to be a government worker.

If you applied after completing your junior year in high school and were successful, you would be able to have five years of study to complete the Baccalaureate Superior Technique (BST). If one waited until completion of Senior High School and if granted a government scholarship, one would have six or seven year of study to become an engineer, doctor, economist or other specialists.

I was in a Junior high school and felt I could not wait to escape Cambodia. I applied for a scholarship to study in a socialist friendship country. I selected East Germany as my first choice. The second were either Czechoslovakia, Hungaria, or Bulgaria and my third choice was the Soviet Union. I asked my cousin Kun Reth who was a public employee; the midwife working for Cambodian-Soviet Friendship Hospital to sponsored my application for studying abroad.

Cousin Reth and his sister, Pov were living with us. They both left their apartment, next to Angkor cinema, behind. My mom provides them daily food. It was a hard burden to our family because mom was the only person who worked to support five people including, my sister, Margaret, Cousin, Reth, Pov and my self. My two cousins were living with us started from 1985 after my brother, Reagan left for the Soviet Union. My super mom was a good-hearted person.

My scholarship application had to successfully move from 'Sangkat', the sub-district level, to 'Khan', the district level, including the civil administration and police departments of each level. The authorities at each level had to certify that I was a good citizen with good morals and a perfect record that the communist required.

The discipline council and communist youth alliance committee still had not approved my application for the Communist Youth Alliance (CYA). Therefore, in my application, I could not state that I was a CYA member "samachek sompon yuvachhun" because my application was still pending. I was therefore sure that my chance of receiving a scholarship was very slim.

In order to obtain each signature and get a good certification from each level authority, I had to have a small gift--one small cigarette package with one thousand riel which equals three or four dollars--to both civil and police administration officials.

It had become a common practice so that if one did not have any money or cigarette gift attached, the application would never get past with a good certification or would obtain a bad record and the process would take forever.

Everyone knew that the civil and police administration officials had a very low salary scale. They also needed to survive. Therefore, they had to use their authority to obtain money by whatever means they could in order to feed their family.

Every week, I rode my bicycle to the Department of Education to see if I find my name on the list. I discussed this with Chorvivan, Chesda, Sambat, Sundara, Pheng, Sovanna, Chamroeun, Khema and especially my closest friend, Chhim Sokhunvireak. He was also my next-door neighbor. We talked about why we needed to apply for a scholarship now and why we didn't wait until after we finished high school.

My friends and I also applied for scholarships to become military air fighters or helicopter pilots. But after receiving medical check-ups by Russian military recruiters, all of us were disqualified due to health, vision or height requirements.

Even though we were qualified to study to become military tank and artillery operators in the Socialist Republic of Vietnam, we knew we didn't want to go where we would not have enough food to eat.

Definitely, if you studied military science in the Socialist Republic of Vietnam (SRV) and when you returned to Cambodia, you would be promoted to captain and have more privileges than those who completed their military study in the Soviet Union.

If you studied for the military in the Soviet Union and returned to Cambodia, you would be promoted to the rank of Second Lieutenant, you would not have the privileges like those from (SRV). We were not concerned with position and title, we only worried about the standard of living of the country we would be in and whether or not we would have enough food to eat. We knew the Soviet Union was good in that regard and that the Socialist Republic of Vietnam was not.

Vireak and I had similar ideas. We decided to apply immediately because first, neither of us had any government connection and second, if we waited until we finished high school, our chances of getting a scholarship would be even smaller since there would be lots of students applying at that time.

Vireak and I normally played together, including table tennis, football and volleyball. Vireak's mother knew my family very well. His family was better off financially than mine.

His brother-in-law was a pharmacist, one of the senior communist positions for the Ministry of Public Health in 1982. When he and his family escaped to the Thai's border for re-settling in France, the government was very angry. They seized all family property and dismissed all privileges that his family had enjoyed. This was the "Sivphov Kama Pibal", known as the book of Kama Pibal, and included a mini car, an apartment and other properties. In addition, the government also accused the remaining family members of betraying the revolution of the people's communist party.

Everyday, I dreamed of studying in a socialist friendship country. I visited the Soviet Cultural Center every Sunday to see a movie or a documentary film and also learn the Russian language. The Eastern European communist bloc countries had no cultural centers in Cambodia. Every time, I saw a documentary film about the technology and development in Russia, I felt so excited and happy. I continued to compare the Soviet Union to heaven.

In high school, I choose Russian as the language to study rather than Vietnamese. I was always a straight "A" student in my Russian class.

One day, our teacher was sick so there was no class. There were probably around 10 of us with bicycles and we went to see the movie at Vehearntip Cinema. The theater was located on Monivong

Boulevard, near the East German Embassy. We parked, pay the fee for our bicycles and got our tickets. We all went into the cinema and got our seats in one of the middle rows. First there was a documentary film before the movie started. When the real movie titled "The Russian Military Youth" started, suddenly, there were people running from the back row and shouting "Chap Tirhean, Chap Tirhean, Chap Tirhean" which meant the military was capturing and forcing young men to join the army services.

In this cinema there were only three exits, one in the back and the other two on the left and right sides. We knew that in the back there would be a military truck, parked in front of the exit. We saw about ten to fifteen men with AK-47s. We, all of my friends and I, panicked and we ran out to the left exit. There were three soldiers there, but they were pushed by the runners and fell down on the ground without having a chance to open fire. Normally, they opened fire toward those who tried to escape. They did not fire toward us because that they had orders not to shoot people because it was in mid-town and there was a friendship socialist bloc embassy in the area. They just fired into the air to threaten people so that they could capture them.

That was why we could escape and not be forced to be in the armed services. Fortunately, this was a good situation for us to run. We all ran in every direction. Chavivon and I ran to the next building and hid there. One good family asked us why we ran and we replied, "Chap Tirhean." They could see that there were a lot of soldiers with a truck outside. My friends had scattered everywhere. We didn't know where they were. This family allowed my friend and me to hide in their home.

Two hours later, the military truck left. The situation around that area was quiet. People were scared of going out of their homes. We waited another hour just to check and see how things were before we returned to the cinema to pick up our bicycles.

Three hours later, this good family told us that the military had left the area. Chavivon and I thanked them for allowing us to hide there and returned to the cinema to pick up our bicycles. I was so happy because I saw my bicycle was there. Unfortunately, Chavivon bicycle was gone. The army took it because his bicycle was a foreign made one, known as a "miyata bicycle" which was considered the best, a quality bicycle. The army took all the new and foreign-made bicycles. We considered these communist soldiers to be robbers.

I took Chavivon to his home at the Olympic market on my bicycle. As we went we were afraid there would be a checkpoint to capture young men and force them to be in the army.

Finally, we arrived at his home and he asked me to stay with him. I told him "no" that I had to go home because my mom was waiting for me. If I did not get home, she would be worried and would not sleep at all.

The international community was putting high pressure on the Vietnamese. With the initiatives of the Indonesian Minister of Foreign Affairs, Mochtar Kusumaatmadja, who was chairman of the ASEAN Standing Committee in December 1978, and later his successor, Ali Alatas, the ASEAN countries played a central role in peaceful negotiations between Cambodia and Vietnam.

With the help of Indonesian president Sue Hato who used to be friends with King Norodom Sihanouk, the government of Indonesia played a major role to bring peace and stability to Cambodia as well as to the region. The first Jarkata Informal Meeting (JIM-1) was held in the Indonesian capital and involved with all of parties concerned: Cambodia, Vietnam, Indonesia and others Asian countries.

As Cambodian children, we never saw western foreigners in our country during the People's Republic of Kampuchea (PRK). The PRK did not allow any western foreigners to enter. We saw only the Russians and Vietnamese experts.

The Russians helped the PRK in most fields, medical and technical. The Russians has sent their doctors to work and cooperate with Cambodian doctors in the Cambodian-Soviet Friendship

Hospital, which was built with free-donations from the Soviet Union during the early sixtys, the Sangkum Reas Niyum regime, the time when King Sihanouk was the head of state. This hospital was one of the biggest hospitals in Cambodia at that time.

For technical assistance, the Russians sent their professors to teach in the Cambodian-Soviet Friendship Institute for Technology and Poly-Technique. This institute was also built with donations from the Soviet Union during the sixtys. This Poly-Technique Institute is one of the biggest educational institutions in Cambodia. The institute conducted the education and study in the Russian language until 1992.

Students who wanted to study in this institute to be Baccalaureate Superior Technique (BST) or an engineer had to pass the entrance exam. The first year, students had to study the Russian language then the second year, they could start studying their subject area.

Chorvivan, Chesda, Sambat, Sundara, Pheng, Sovanna, Chamroeun, Khema, especially Po Sreang, and Sokhunvireak and I were always talking about why we did not see any Americans or other westerners helping in Cambodia.

We also discussed why we did not see any American donations of any kind toward medical or technical assistance in our country. We used to hear that the Americans were rich, powerful and kind but we saw no evidence of it.

That's why, after our assessment, my friends and I agreed that this could lead King Sihanouk who was the head of state during the Sangkum Reas Niyum Regime, toward the communist because the communists helped us and the capitalists didn't.

Near where I lived in Phnom Penh, probably around half a mile away, there was the Cambodia Railway Station, built in 1936, during the French colonial period. The train runs from Phnom Penh to the northwest, Battambang province and to Sihanoukville, a seashore province.

Every time the train arrived, we saw lots of people coming out of the station; some carrying chickens, ducks, pigs and rice. They put them on small carts so that they could   sell them in Phnom Penh city. Some mini businessmen hired soldiers to accompany them to avoid being hassled by the military and police.

Normally, the military and police with 4 to 6 people sitting and waiting on their Russian-Made Military Tri-Motorcycles (motorcycle with three wheels) set up check points at the corner roads between the USSR Boulevard and street 109 toward Psar Dimech market every time the train arrived. They tried to confiscate all of the commodities that the communist government banned. The clash, small arms fire exchange between the mini businessmen's soldiers and the city military and police, at least for an hour became normal.

I could see clearly from the second floor of my apartment all of this activity. Sometimes the military and police used their tri-motorcycle to chase the mini businessmen accompanied by their hired soldiers who used the motorcycle cart (motorcycle attached to a small trailer) which carried all kinds of commodities- foodstuff and canned food products, rice, expensive clothes, other materials.

The military and police would normally fire up into the air first and if they did not stop, they started firing toward the people. They all drove fast to escape from the military and police while exchanging fire back toward the police to scare them not to follow and chase them any longer. These commodities and products normally were brought in from Thailand.

The People's Republic of Kampuchea (PRK) 1987-1988
My Life in Another Communist PRK regime

At this time my sister Margaret and I were in Senior High School. We both were excited that we had only one more year before we could enter University.

In Cambodia during the People's Republic of Kampuchea (PRK) period, there were only two hotels open to the foreign public--one was the Monorom Hotel and the second one was the Samaki Hotel. The Monorom was the hotel where the PRK's government allowed foreigners from friendship socialist countries to stay. Sometimes we Cambodians saw a few western capitalist foreigners there as well due to rooms are full in Samaki Hotel. The Samaki Hotel was the place the PRK's government allowed only foreigners who came from western capitalist countries to stay.

This made the PRK's government's secret agents job easier to do their spy and investigations if there were any contacts with local people. Once, on a Thursday when my school class was off, two of my friends and I went to the national library, which was located near Wat Phnom and Hotel Samaki. This was the first time that my friends, Porsreang, Sunleang and I saw an elder priest dressed in a long black robe. His name was Father Nazarine, he said, and he came from California, in a capitalist country of the United States of America and was staying in the Samaki hotel. We all were excited to have an opportunity to practice our English language with him in the park in front of the hotel. He gave each one of us his name card.

We had forgotten that we were not allowed to talk with foreigners. We sat in the park and practiced our English with him. We tried to understand what he said to us in an American accent. We asked him to tell us about America. We told him that we, Cambodians, considered most western people and countries like America as heaven. What we meant was that the prosperous countries and her people had all their basic needs met. In the conversation with him, I showed him my gold cross necklace that Mom made for me.

In fact, I just wore this necklace to keep myself from evil. Based on what Mom said, if you had gold or diamonds on you, your star was high and would be protected from any evil spirit who might want to enter you. The most important thing, in case of an emergency, I could sell or exchange it for food to survive. If I were captured by the military or police to force me to join the army and fight against the Khmer Rouge, I could use this to bribe them to escape.

We continued our conversation with him for about two hours. By noon he told us that he had to go back into the hotel so we said good-bye. Then we all left for home. We walked to different destinations. I walked home from Samaki hotel through Monivong Boulevard, turned left on USSR Boulevard and then turned toward Street 109.

It was then that I noticed one person following me. I was kind of nervous and did not know what to do. I decided not to go home because I was afraid first he might learn my home address. I believed the person who followed me was a PRK secret agent. If he know my address, he might capture me any time. Therefore, I decided to walk toward the Wat Koh School.

I walked faster and then began to run. I ran for quite sometime and then I stopped for a minute just to check if he was still following me. I knew when I started running he was also running. This indicated that he absolutely was a government secret agent. I had a good opportunity when I arrived at Wat Koh School. I looked back and I did not see him. It was during a recess for students so there were lots of students hanging out and playing on the playground. I started hiding myself in the crowd of students.

I was so nervous and afraid. I started talking to God, "Please, God, help me, please God help me to escape from this!"

I went to the back of the school and started to jump up over the school fence. I looked up to the left and right to see if there was still someone following me. Thank God. The agent had disappeared!

When I arrived home, I just took a bath and went to sleep with fear on my mind. Before sleeping, I started to think, to review and look back on all of the situations that had happened to me. I had escaped from many dangerous things, starting with the Khmer Rouge to the PRK regime. I realized that there must be an angel who was watching over me and who always helped me from behind the scenes.

I began to really pray to the Lord my God every day and night, especially when big problems came.

That year, I applied once again for a scholarship to study in a Friendship Socialist Country. The civil administration and police, Sangkat, sub district and Khan district, by now knew me very well through my visits to their office nearly every day just to follow up and check the status of my application. They said straight to me, "To help us process your application faster we need speed up fee with additional services fee." This was not considered a government fee. It was just a tip or some kind of tea/coffee/Chinese noodle money for them.

It was during this time that I found out that my application to become a communist youth alliance member was still pending. Therefore, in my scholarship application, I could not state that I was a CYA member. If my application for the communist youth was approved, I would have a better chance to receive a scholarship, at least to Mongolia or Cuba. If I were lucky enough I might even have a chance to have a scholarship to the Soviet Union.

Most Cambodian students wanted to escape the country during these times of hunger and poverty.

The next day, when I was in school, my friend Sundara who had a brother who worked for the secret services "Sar Mpey Muy" known as S21 Department, told him to tell me that for my security, I must stop talking to foreigners from capitalist countries. If not if I were captured, I would be sent to a children's correction department for conspiracy against the People's Republic of Kampuchea. This bad news made me scared and afraid. There were different secret services, some from S21 and others from S23 Department, know in Khmer as "Sar Mpey Bey". The S23 was the most powerful during the PRK.

I also had a friend name Phanareth. His brother worked for the PRK council of ministers. He also was the head of Monorom Hotel. When there were days off from school, I always went to play with him at the Monorom Hotel. Through my connection with him, I was allowed to play in the hotel. This hotel accepted only foreigners from communist friendship countries.

Samaki Hotel was the one where only foreigners from capitalist countries were accepted. One day, I had a chance to speak to a foreigner again but I felt it was OK because I knew that it would not give me any problem since foreigners who stay at Monorom are from communist countries that were PRK friendship countries. While having a conversation with him, he told me that he was a German from West Germany. I was kind of surprised that this was the second time I could meet someone from a western country. He told me that he could bring me to live with him in his country. I was so happy but nervous and wondered if it was true and if he was a good person. I asked him to wait for me so I could go home and tell my mother (Mom) about this and get her permission before I went with him.

I asked him how he could take me with him to West Germany. He told me that he would put me in a wooden box. He told me that I would have to sit or sleep in the box in the cargo plane section.

When we arrived in a foreign land he would open the box and I could sit in the airplane seat next to him after that. If not, he would open the box for me when we arrived in his country. I asked my friend Phanareth and he said that it would be OK and he would not tell anyone about this.

There were a few Cambodians who left the country this way. The capitalist foreigners said they adopted the Cambodians and the best way to take them out of the country was to put them into a wooden box with a bribe to the PRK communist officer in charge. I also wondered if these foreigner capitalists were good people. Ninety nine percent of the time, people thought only of how to get out of the country, not thinking about what life would be like when they arrived in the foreign place.

I grew up seeing many people killed and tyrannized through violence, poverty, anger and hunger. My anger and revenge were always in my mind. I always asked why our leaders killed our own people? Why our leaders did not take good care our people and our country? Why do we not unite and work together? Why our leaders do not attempt to eliminate hunger and poverty? Why our leaders do not reconstruct and rebuild our country especially, national roads that could link the entire country with electricity and clean water.

I wondered why a person wanted to be prime minister or a top leader by being a puppet and being installed by a foreign ruler like the Vietcong, the Socialist Republic of Vietnamese (SRV) who gave them orders of what to do and what not to do. The puppet has to do everything for his master, including killing his own people, giving part of our land and ocean to the foreign masters, taking good care of these people of the foreign ruler by giving them many privileges. Foreign master people have strong support from the PRK's government. This government has to accept thousands and thousands of illegal foreign ruler people to live and offer them privileges in our country.

In return, the puppet gets strong support in everything to guarantee that he can stay in power for the rest of his life if he follows and obeys the orders from the foreign master, now the Vietnamese communists.

My childhood friend, Vireak, who was also my next-door neighbor, was my normal playmate. After school and during free time, we both played football and table tennis. I also played and competed in the national table tennis competition.

Every weekend after helping mom with sales at the Oressey market, Vireak and I would go to the home of Mr. Chhea Thang. He was Vice Minister of Public Health during the People's Republic of Kampuchea's regime. He liked to play table tennis with his son, Theh. Mr. Chea Thang was a tall and good man. He also played badminton in Bloc Seng Thai building where Vireak and I lived.

We all practiced table tennis for the national competition.

During this year, the Vietnamese troops continued to partially withdrew from Cambodia due to international pressure. The PRK government always celebrated any big event by asking students throughout the major cities to line the streets with flags. Students in all schools in Phnom Penh were off for one day. We were ordered to stand on the roadside and express our thanks to the Vietnamese troops who were leaving the country. Normally, after the Vietnamese troops left the country, they were ordered to return in secret. This was just a show for the international arena to believe that the Vietnamese government withdrew their troops from Cambodia.

Friends introduced me to a group of children who parents were in PRK's politburo and communist standing committees. They told me that they had just returned from living and studying in East Germany. They said they did not know how to live there since everything was completely different from Cambodia. They reported that everything was good and progressive including roads, electricity, water and beautiful buildings. These children faced a new environment, geography and culture.

Therefore, they decided to return to Cambodia because here their lifestyle and way of living was easy. They could do anything they wanted. It was completely different for us. We, normal people, had to worry about where our next meal would come from. What were we going to do when this food was gone? All of my friends said these communist children were foolish. They did not know what was right and what was wrong. What were valuable, good and what was not? My friends and I were so excited to have a conversation with these communist children about East Germany. Our conversation went on and on until they were tired of us.

My friends and I were with these communist children for the whole day. We played together in the villa in Toul Kork area.

My friends and I wanted to associate with them because we wanted a connection to the government. We thought they might help us through their parents with a connection to our scholarships to study in friendship socialist countries.

Once I had an opportunity to see a friend off at the Pochentong International Aiport. Pathey was my schoolmate. She was in class "D" and I was in class "C". I got up early and rode my bicycle to the Department of Education. When I arrived there on my bicycle, I saw lot of students. I locked my bicycle to the metal pole and walked into the department. Most of students were dressed in white shirt, blue or black pants with a tie, jacket or suit. She approached me and introduced me to her family and friends. I felt out of place because I did not know anyone besides her. All of the students that had been selected and won a scholarship to study in friendship socialist countries had a strong governmental connection.

She won a scholarship to study in Bulgaria for five years. Her brother in law sponsored her. He was a military division commander of the PRK regime. Military Division Commanders were considered one of the highest communist officials. That is why she was selected to study in one of the best socialist countries like Bulgaria.

The procedure was simple. When you won a scholarship to study in any of the friendship socialist countries, the PRK Cambodian Red Cross helped you. This organization provided two pair of warm used clothes and ties per student to protect you from the cold and snow when you were there.

She excused herself from me and went to her family and friends. Now all families and friends of the students had to wait in a different area. The officer of educational department called the students by name. Today, there were a lot of students who went to study in all friendship socialist countries. The announcement went on and on. Some were to the Soviet Union, East Germany, Bulgaria, Hungary, Poland, Czechoslovakia, Mongolia and Cuba. Finally, I heard "Soun Pathey, student candidate for the People's Republic of Bulgaria". Please move forward to the Educational Department vehicle for the airport.

At that point I started feeling so sad. I pitied myself. I felt like crying but I didn't because I was in public. At last, the educational officer instructed the friends and family to get on a vehicle to Pochengton International Airport.

The convoy of students' vehicles was moving first then the convoy for friends and family followed it. All first vehicles were full of students who went to study in friendship socialist countries.

Arriving at Pochengton International Airport, I got out of the vehicle. I saw only one big Russian plane "Aeroflot" on the airport field waiting for these students to go onboard. There were no planes except this giant one. There were no other passengers on this plane. This plane was only for students who went to study abroad. The flight would leave Cambodia to Vietnam for transit, later, to India or Karachi for a second transit then finally to the Soviet Union. It was unbelievable. The whole Pochengton International Airport during the PRK regime was limited to these planes. This was evidence that the PRK regime cut off their relationships to the rest of the capitalist world.

Now students started saying good-bye to their family, friends, boy and girl friends before they went onboard. I could not see Pathey since the place was crowded full of students and families.

First were the student candidates for the Soviet Union then continued till the last for Cuba and Mongolia?

Finally, I saw Pathey waive to me while walking forward to the Officer to receive her passport. It had been arranged by the department of education with the ministry of foreign affairs. She paused and waived to me again before she walked up to the plane.

A person standing next to me started up a conversation with me. He said that normally each student passport was held and kept by one person who was the educational department officer representative who traveled with them. It was kind of a surprise that this time, they circulated and give each passport to the holder.

Now we heard the giant Russian plane "Aeroflot" made its noise for taking off into the air.

All of the students' families, friends, including myself, looked up at the Russian plane "Aeroflot" in the sky until it disappeared in the horizon. Now, we all got in the department of education vehicle going back to Phnom Penh.

After arriving in Phnom Penh at the Department of Education, I unlocked my bicycle from the pole and rode home. I took a bath and cried, feeling sadness for myself because I did not have an opportunity like others to study in friendship socialist countries. And I did not know what my life was going to be?

That night, I dreamed of studying in one of the friendship socialist countries. In my dream, I saw I could escape from many checkpoints that were installed by the PRK armies to capture young men and force them to join the army and fight against the Khmer Rouge.

When I got up the next day morning, I started doing an assessment and evaluation of my dream. I thought once again that I must have an angel watching over me and protecting me all the time.

For example, there were a serious and big fighting between the Khmer Rouge troops and the Vietnamese forces with the cooperation from PKK's armies by firing rockets, bombs, and machine guns. Bullets flew everywhere like rain drops but I just lay down on the ground and I was safe. It was unbelievable. But it was true.

During the Khmer Rouge period I was punished for escaping from the village. I refused to join the children's mobile team concentration camp. The chief of the children's mobile team with the assistance from the local militia chased me into the deep forest and captured me. She tyrannized, hit, stabbed me with a stick, and tried to force me to kill myself. I had to dig a hole which was to be my grave while the guard of the local militia held an AK-47 rifle on me. When I finished digging, he would use his AK – 47 riffle to kill me or just put me into that hole and bury me alive.

While I was digging the earth, the super-natural happened. In the forest where I was digging, the big branch of a palm tree fell down and hit the local militia who was guarding me. He lost consciousness so I could escape.

Without invisible help like this and the help of the good Khmer Rouge people themselves, I might be dead ten or twenty times already. The good thing, throughout my childhood, if anything was going to happen to me, my angel always gave me some kind of sense that I knew in advance that something was going to happen to me. So I had to prepare myself to be ready in thinking ahead, planning a tactic for escape.

We Cambodians are people of peace and kindness with good-hearts, high-dignity, and respect for one another. But through out the civil war and the conflict between the east and the west ideology-communist and capitalists, especially in Pol Pot and PRK's regimes these values were lost. The Khmer Rouge and PRK regimes completely destroyed the trust and kindness that most everyone had. People during these times were more selfish and thought only about themselves. There were many people who lived on other people's suffering by exploiting and oppressing them.

I still was confused about what kind of God would send his angels to watch over and protect me. I was a Buddhist but I always wanted to be a Christian Protestant. I loved my gold cross necklace that Mom made for me. I wore it all the time, everywhere I went because I believed that if I had my cross necklace with me, it meant that God was with me. I don't know where this idea came from.

I knew very little about being a Christian. King Sihanouk was the head of state and the Khmer Republic, Marshal Lon Nol, the head of government. During the Lon Lol regime there was one Christian church in Phnom Penh. If you attended the church, they would provide you with food. Church people were also very helpful for one another without classes. That church was on Monivong Boulevard. It was on the opposite side of the street from the Samaki Hotel. The Khmer Rouge destroyed the church during their time of ruling the country. All that is left now is just the body of the stone building that is scattered everywhere. That was the limit of my knowledge about Christians.

The People's Republic of Kampuchea (PRK) 1989-1990
My Life to the Glimpse and Sunrise

The 1987-1988 academic year was the final exam year for my sister Margaret and I in High School. We both were kind of nervous and anxious about the coming examination. The day before it was to take place, we went to look at the exam center. The Ministry of Education and the Department of Education classified students by family name. Since I used my father's family name, my last name starts with Am, so I was assigned to the children school center, known in Khmer as "Mondul sala komarey".

For my sister, she had a different family name from me. She goes by my mother's last name, which starts with KIM so her exam was scheduled in Bak Touk High School Center, known as "Mondul sala Bak Touk". That day, we were so excited to have an opportunity to ride in a car with my friends, Chorvivan, Chesda, Sambat, Phannarith, Sna and Dy. Chorvivan's family was rich during the PRK because his family had strong connections with the PRK government. His family had a European car, a yellow Mercedes. He took all of us to the center to look for our names on the billboard. We finally found our names then we proceeded to see the exact room where the exam would take place for each of us.

After seeing our names and the room, we all got into Chorvivan's Mercedes and he drove us around for sightseeing. We saw the Independence Monument, known as "Vimean Ekreak", the riverside, "tam mutonle" and we stopped at the Royal Palace. We all had fried noodles with beef, egg and green vegetable and a soybean soft drink. I felt so lucky to have a good friend like Chorvivan. He was nice and kind to all our friends. He paid the cost for everything. He made me so happy that day. I had never before had an opportunity to ride in a Mercedes. Sambat's father worked for the Ministry of Public Work in the PRK's government. Chorvivan's father was a businessman and had links to the PRK government. Most of my friends did not have a father because our fathers had been killed by the Pol Potist's. These were the only two friends that had their fathers alive--Sambat and Chorvivan. During my senior year I made new friends because I transferred to study in a different school, Toul Kork High School. Chorvivan and I were the closest friends.

The next day we took the examination. Two weeks later, after the correction by the examination committees, the Department of Education announced the results. All of my friends, Chorvivon, Sambat, Chesda, Phannarith, Sophea, Bunna, Hun, Rith, Sna and Dy and also my sister, Margaret and I were so happy that this year, we all passed the final Senior High School Examination. Finally, Margaret and I had completed our study in Senior High School. During the People's Republic of Kampuchea (PRK), students had to pass the exam in order to complete High School so that they could continue and take the entrance exam to the university.

Now, my friends and I faced another challenge. Some of my friends decided to take the entrance exam to go to local universities. Others, like me, decided to take both the local exam while waiting for a scholarship to study in one of the friendship socialist countries. Most of my friends did not pass the entrance exam to study in local universities or receive a scholarship. This was not because they were not good students but because of the corrupt system and the pressures of our political society. Through connections Sambat received an opportunity to go to law school. During the People's Republic of Kampuchea (PRK) regime, the law school just had an associate's degree but the economics department had a full bachelor's degree. Most of the professors at both places were Vietnamese. The PRK government had signed a treaty with the People's Socialist Republic of Vietnam concerning Educational Cooperation and Assistance therefore; the two educational institutions had Vietnamese professor to teach Khmer students.

For the technical university, we had Russian professors to teach. After passing an entrance exam, the first year students had to study the Russian language because all of the courses were taught in Russian.

Every day I rode my bicycle to the Department of Education, which was located in the district of Sangkat Boeung Keng Kang. I went to find out the results of my scholarship application to the friendship socialist countries in Eastern Europe. Because of my frequent visits, most of the public employees of this educational department became familiar with me and called me by name. They told me that if I wanted to receive a scholarship, I needed to have connections. If not, I would have to bribe or have something for an official in exchange for a scholarship. My family was poor so we did not have an ability to do that.

I was facing many problems. My first problem was that I was not only unable to receive a scholarship to study in a friendship socialist country in Eastern Europe but also I could not continue my higher education in a local university because of the corrupt educational system. The second was that I was going to be forced to join the army because by law under the PRK regime, each family had to have at least one member of their family serving in the PRK's army.

During that time I was hardly ever able to see my old high school friends. We were out of school and I missed them and my school very much. Some began their own business ventures, other started having a job as government employees-Phnom Penh City and Traffic Police but I didn't know what some of the others were doing.

End of 1990 my brother and his team completed their study in the former Soviet Union, the Union of Soviet Socialist Republics. None of Cambodia's students who studied in the friendship socialist countries wanted to return home after the completion of their education. This included my brother, Reagan.

That year, Reagan and his team were sent back home after their study was completed. They all arrived in Phnom Penh by the Russian Aeroflot airline. I was happy to see Reagan. He had become so handsome. He was healthy and tall with light skin. He did not talk much and seemed quieter than I remembered him to be. He missed Russia because in Cambodia we did not have enough food to eat. He started to worry and was often sad and depressed because he wanted to return to Russia.

With the help of my mother and the help of our neighbor, Mr. Sring and Mrs Chhiv, Reagan was assigned to work for the Ministry of Industry in the capital city of Phnom Penh. After six months of this duty, Reagan was reassigned first to work at Governmental Kampuchea Electrical Inc., next to Watt Phnom Pagoda and latter to First Kampuchea Electrical Manufacturer, next to national old stadium. Because we lacked government connections he was reassigned from one place to another.

1989 and 1990 was a crucial year for my family. Mom's business did not go well. Mom was having to support six of us--three of my cousins, Bon Reth, Bon Pov and Bon Pros and my brother, Reagan, sister, Margaret and myself. Reagan's salary was around 4000 riels, which equals one U.S dollar and twenty cents and government assistant with 10 kilogram of rice per month. This didn't provide us enough to eat.

Because I did not pass the local university entrance exam nor receive a scholarship to study abroad, my life had ended up here. Every day and night, I had to think of ways to help mom and my family to have a better life. Therefore, I decided to use my little knowledge of the English language that I had studied secretly for many years to transfer this knowledge for the mutual benefit of the younger generation and myself. Every day, I was worried, sad and depressed. But there was a superior power in my mind that I had to think positively. I had to believe that positive thinking would produce positive results.

I decided to rent a classroom at Watt Koh and Phnom Daun Penh School. I talked to both school directors and everything went smoothly. The decision was that the rent would be 38% percent of my total income from teaching English. This fee included classroom space and electricity. As you probably know, during the PRK regime, electricity was on and off frequently. Sometimes we did not have electricity at all. But I had my own oil lamp, which used oil and pressure, known as "chanh keang mangsong" to light my classroom when the electricity was down. We mostly did not have electricity.

I had to find an artist with painting skills to create my signs. The sign needed to include the kind of English class (beginning or intermediate), when it was going to start (date and time), and where the class would be held (school and classroom number). At that time, I needed to pay only for the sign. Finally, the sign was done and I wanted to post it on a long wall close to the two schools to advertise my class. Every day, I went to check the sign and make sure it was in good shape. Sometimes, bad kids tore it down and we had to make a new one. This made me mad because I did not have money to pay for multiple signs. My class schedule was the first session for new beginners, Essential English Book One, 11:30am-12: 30am, second session for Essential English Book Two, 12:30pm-1: 30pm and in the evening first session for new beginners, Essential English Book One, 5:30pm-6: 30pm, second session for Essential English Book Two, 6:30pm-7:30pm. Therefore, I was to teach four hours a day.

The announcement for the English class took place three week in advance of the start date for the class. During these three weeks, I was busy doing my own preparation for my two classes. It was very helpful that I had my own notes from when I had studied these books, from book I, II, III and IV as a student. As a part of my preparation, I visited different English classes to learn new techniques from different English teachers and to see how they presented themselves. I wanted to learn how they began each lesson and maintained the students' attention. For me, the beginning was one of the most difficult parts to do.

The day of my two English classes arrived. I was kind of nervous and pleasantly surprised to see that my first season class had around 30 students registered, including boys and girls, young adults, adults and middle aged students. I was so excited to see them. A part of that excitement was that I thought I would make lots of money.

On the first day, I stood by the door to greet them. Most of them asked me where the teacher was. I told them to please make themselves at home, find a seat, and that the teacher would be with us soon. They did not know that I was their teacher. They kept asking me and were curious to know who I was.

Finally, the clock turned 11:30. I started to introduce myself to them and welcome them to my English class and the book Essential English Book I for new beginners. I told them that I was their teacher. I introduced myself to them and gave them my thorough background. Most of them whispered to each other, "Gee, this teacher is so young." I told them the rules and procedures for the class. In return, I asked each of them to introduce themselves to the class, giving their name, school and work.

One of the older students, Sary, was very helpful. We seemed to have a connection when we met each other for the first time. He helped me to collect my fee during the middle hour of the class. I charged 500 riels per hour, which equals about 20 US cents. I was also fortunate to have two students whom parents were in the politburo member of the People's Republic of Kampuchea (PRK) and Chairman of the Cambodian-Vietnamese Friendship Communist Highest Organization and one doctor.

When we finished the introductions, I told them that on this first day we would study about greetings in English. We learned how to use "Good Morning," "Good Afternoon," and "Good Evening," as well as "How are you?" "How do you do?" "What is your name?" and "See you tomorrow." And "Goodbye." I explained when it was appropriate to use each of these. I wrote these on the black board with Cambodian translations. I gave them around ten minutes to copy them down, and then I asked the class to repeat after me. Finally, we did role-plays by pretending one person was local and the other one was a foreigner from a different country.

At first, I felt very nervous to see these students who were mostly older than me. After talking and explaining for five to ten minutes however, I started feeling great and proud to be a teacher with lots of students in class.

1990 was a little bit better than other years. It seemed like an opening for the PRK to reform--the PRK perestroyka. We saw a few capitalist foreigners from western countries walk on the streets. We local people could speak with them. I tried to make friends with those tourists and invited them to visit my English class. I asked them to give me advice and feedback to improve my teaching. The visits of foreign tourists to my English class helped me to have more students who wished to study with me. Most Cambodian students wanted to practice their English language skills with native English speakers.

I also continued to study English myself to improve my knowledge and ability. I had several famous teachers. Mr. Tha who was a government police officer was one of them. He was known as the master of English Grammar. Mr. Thach San who was chief newspaper editor and Mr. Peng Ly who were the national radio chief editor and speaker were others. I collected the techniques and experiences from these famous teachers and established my own standards of teaching.

I realized that I did not have a degree to teach but I had the ability to do it and that was considered a great resource for me. But I had a problem of when I introduced myself as an English teacher, the students would asked me what school I went to. I told them that I had studied the English language since I was young. My first teacher was a woman who used to work for the U.S Embassy and Agency for international development. Now she was in Australia.

The second, Mr. Somalin, the third Mr. Sokhom, Mr. Thach San, Mr. Tha and it went on and on. I studied in a secret school under the communists. Therefore, we did not have an official name for the school.

My star and living standards were rising little by little. After teaching my class, I enjoyed having Chinese food and other things I had never eaten before. This was the first time I had plenty of food to eat. Some of the money from my teaching went to my mother to help our family with daily living needs. Some I kept for myself and the rest went for rent to the two school directors.

With my history of being an English teacher and the experiences I had had negotiating good relations with the school directors, I offered to help my brother to rent space at these schools for him to teach English as well. I helped him to make a sign as an advertisement before his class started. Everything went well for him. The school directors of Wat Koh School agreed for him to have his class on the second floor of the building and next to mine. When the day came, Reagan had lots of students as well.

I knew that the country was going to change. Every day, I prepared myself for the university. I knew that my life would be rising again. As the saying goes, "When the water rises, the fish eat ants; when the water falls, the ants eat fish." I believed that I would have an opportunity to have my dream of higher education come true one day.

Under the People's Republic of Kampuchea, a communist regime installed by the Socialist Republic of Vietnam, most of the Cambodian people, including my family, had little to eat. Most of us suffered from malnutrition. My family and I had never been satiated with food. Even though this was tough, it was far better than when we were under the Khmer Rouge regime. The PRK regime did not kill people like the Khmer Rouge did. Under the PRK, the ways the people were killed were completely different. They forced young men and older men to clear out the forests, which were full of land mines. People would get killed easily because of the frequent mine explosions or sometimes the Khmer Rouge would fire on them from an ambush and kill them.

The PRK government also forced people to join the army and sent them out to the battlefield along the Thai border to fight against the Khmer Resistance Forces, which were supported by the Americans. During the cold war there were two giant super powers, one was the Soviet Union and the other one was the United States of America.

Under the PRK we never seemed to have enough food available for the country's population even thought it was far better than the Khmer Rouge. The government controlled all of the food supplies. Everything was in the hands of the government. There was a minor private business sector, which was allowed to operate during the PRK before the reform. During the PRK government people were not allowed to travel from one place to another without a permit from the local authority. No one was allowed to go out beyond the areas where one was assigned to live. My family lived in the capital city Phnom Penh after the Khmer Rouge regime fell down. We never had a chance to go anywhere outside the capital. We had to report to the local authority if we had a family member come over during an emergency.

I began to feel a great deal of anger toward the PRK's communist government. This anger was always in my mind, heart and soul. I asked myself, how could the communist leaders treat their own people like a wild animals, even worst than domestic cats and dogs are treated in western countries. Every day, my anger grew bigger and stronger.

I asked my super mom to help me. I told her to please sell all of her valuable gold and use the money to bribe the PRK senior educational department director. In return, I would receive a free scholarship to study in one of the friendship socialist countries. I so wanted to be a doctor or an economist or a military air fighter pilot.

In my mind I thought that if I got a scholarship from the government, then I would have a chance to escape to a western country. My dream plan was that during my study in the Soviet Union to be trained as a military air fighter, I would take a test flight and escape to any western neighboring country when I had the chance.

If this plan didn't work I had a second dream. After six years of studying to be a military air fighter pilot in the Soviet Union I would return to Cambodia. When I got an order from the communist PRK's government to fly and bomb the Khmer Rouge along the Thai-Cambodian border, I would have a chance to take my mom and sister on board on this military air fighter. After that I would bomb the government top leaders' buildings, homes and offices, then I would fly and escape to Thailand, Malaysia or Singapore.

My anger continued to grow and I continued to think and plan. One idea I had was to join the communist army. When I was in the army, the PRK communist government would allow me to carry a gun. After that I would have an opportunity to open fire and kill as many of the communist leaders as I could and then bomb the communist government. I asked myself if I would be able to escape and survive after I did this. I knew the answer was no. Not only would I be put to death but the communist government would kill my whole family too even if they had nothing to do with the deed.

On second thought, I realized that I was afraid that if I joined the PRK army and I did not have a strong military connection, they would probably send me straight to the western part of the country, along the Thai-Cambodian border to fight the Khmer Rouge. There I would be killed quickly by the Khmer Rouge forces and never be able to grow old with my family.

That year, the president of the non-alliance countries, Mr. Romes Chandra, originally from India gave a speech in the Cambodian Olympic Stadium about peace, economic, stability and non-alliance countries benefit for the region. His speech was on television and radio. Most of the students in Phnom Penh were asked to join and congratulate President Chandra at his meeting. My class group was asked to raise the banner. When the banner was raised, everyone could see from a distance the message of congratulations to the president, and a picture of a dove, the symbol of peace, prosperity and happiness.

I was so excited to hear for the first time, a foreigner who was the president of the non- alliance countries speak in English with a Cambodian interpreter, Mr. Kong Keng from the Ministry of Foreign Affair of the People's Republic of Kampuchea (PRK). Mr. Kong Keng was recognized as an educated person who had a deep knowledge of the English language during the PRK.

My super Mom told me that, everything would change one day at a time. She reminded me for example the Khmer Rouge regime failed on January 07, 1979. But before the evil ended, many of the innocent were killed. Thousands and thousands piled up like mountains, including my father, Uncle Son, Uncle Song, and Uncle Krukun, cousin, Ry, cousin Roht, aunt Sin and so on. They all left their children behind. Mom said the evil and the bad regime would soon fall. She said continued evil could not survive forever. Only Justice can survive long in this world. This, she said, was God's law for the world.

That year, with the continuation of international pressure and help and collaboration from Indonesian President Ali Alatas, Prime Minister Hun Sen of the PRK communist government negotiated with King Sihanouk who was also former king and prime minister during the Sangkum Reas Niyum regime. He was at that time head of the tripartite coalition government, Cambodian Resistant supported by western countries which include the Khmer Rouge, Khmer National Liberation Front, later known as Buddhist Liberal Democratic Party and Funcinpec is a French abbreviation for **Front Uni National pour un Cambodge Indépendant, Neutre, Pacifique, et Coopératif**, Front Uni National pour en Cambodge (FUNCINPEC) which translates to "National United Front for an Independent, Neutral, Peaceful, and Cooperative Cambodia."

1989-1990 was a marvelous year! The Paris Peace Accord which was to be signed by all four Cambodian Political Factions, the PRK, the Khmer Rouge, the Buddhist Liberal Democratic Party and FUNCINPEC, National United Front for an Independent, Neutral, Peaceful, and Cooperative Cambodia to end the bloodshed in Cambodia.

The negotiation was continued to the peace process in Cambodia and ended with the complete withdrawal of Vietcong, Vietnamese troops from Kampuchea by early 1991.

As time goes by, it seems I forget everything negative and terrible about the PRK government that they did to our people and my family. I was busy with my job as an English teacher. I started my road map plan of teaching. This kept me very busy to do my research and learning new techniques to improve my teaching. I started expanding my teaching hours. I taught six hours a day. My income from teaching was pretty good and fair.

As a part of self-study, I traveled around the city to find western tourists to talk to and make friends with. I continued to bring American and European tourists to my English class and sometimes, I asked them to teach on my behalf if they were willing to do so.

My friendship with these tourists continued as did my interest and concern for my students. I became better known as a young teacher with lots of students wanting to study with me.

All this helped me increase my daily income to help my family out. Thank God, that my family taught me to have a superior idea. Even though we had nothing, but in my mind, heart and soul, I was fully aware that we were good people and that we would improve our circumstances one day at a time. We were certainly better than these bad communist leaders who seemed to live just to be a burden on our society and put the country into poverty and misery.

We, the innocent people were able to do things better than these evil communist leaders. They abused their power and killed their own people like Pol Pot, Ieng Sary, Khiev Samphan and Nuon Chea. They put the country at risk for poverty, hunger and danger. They were forced to remain calms by seeing their foreign ruler, the Vietnamese, took our territory. These communist leaders thought only of their own small group, their own family's happiness, and let thousands upon thousands of innocent people die everyday. I did not know if there were many reasons behind that, therefore, it forced these top communist leaders to do so.

1990 was the early part of my life going toward the sunrise. I saw a glimpse of the horizon of my life. I knew the light would come. This year was my accomplishment year to earn everything by myself. My family and I had enough food to eat. I was so happy to have an ability to support my family with the income that I had from my English teaching. In addition to that, I was hired temporarily to be a translator and interpreter for some charity and non-governmental organizations who were allowed for the first time to operate in Kampuchea.

When the world seemed unfair, especially in Kampuchea, thousands and thousands of innocent lives ended every day because of torture, hunger, and poverty at the hands of evil Cambodian communist leaders, like Pol Pot. The PRK regime was little better.

In spite of this, I believed that one day a super being would come and help our people, our society and the country from this evil. Then I would be a part of this to help out and contribute to our homeland. I prayed it would happen soon!

The State of Cambodia (SOC) 1991-1992
My Life to the Glimpse and Sunrise

After the Paris Peace Accord was signed by all four Cambodian Political Parties, the civil war in Cambodia ended. The parties included the Buddhist Liberal Democratic Party (BLDP) led by former Prime Minister Son San, the National United Front for an Independent, Neutral, and Peaceful Cooperative (FUNCINPEC), headed by King Sihanouk, the Cambodian People's Party, a communist party, which favored its Vietnamese foreign ruler, led by Chairman Chea Sim who had little power with the real power being his Vice Chairman, Mr. Hun Sen and the Khmer Rouge Party as it known most evil and killer, led by figurehead, Kiev Samphan who had little power with all the power with Pol Pot, Ieng Sary, Nuon Chea, Son Sen and Ta Mok. The People's Republic of Kampuchea (PRK) changed its name to the State of Cambodia (SOC) during this transitional period.

Each of the Khmer Political Parties had their representatives in the Cambodia Supreme National Council (SNC), located in SNC building, Force Commander Office, at the United Nations Transitional Authority in Cambodia (UNTAC) Headquarters.

The United Nations first fact-finding mission was established in Phnom Penh, Cambodia known as the United Nations advance mission in Cambodia (UNAMIC). Later, it changed its name to the United Nations Transitional Authority in Cambodia (UNTAC). The purpose of this mission was to set up a general free and fair election in Cambodia to end the civil war caused by different ideologies between the capitalists and socialists.

My sister Margaret won a scholarship to study in the Former Soviet Union but she did not want to study there because after the fall of the Soviet Union, the scholarship was not enough for food, living expense and studying cost. My mom wanted to change this scholarship to my name, therefore mom asked me to talk directly to the senior educational officer in the department of education and tell him that we would give them up to five chi of gold (which equaled about US$250), if they could help us out. Two hundred fifty dollars was too little because they had to distribute a portion to each officer. It just wasn't enough. Because of a very low salary, everyone try to survive. Therefore, they have to do this. They required from eight hundred to one thousand dollars to make such a change. This was impossible for us therefore our plan was not successful.

With the State of Cambodia (SOC) established, things changed. There were students from different universities who held demonstrations against the Cambodia Communist Ruling Party, the CPP, who ran the government at that time. Students from the Faculty of Medicine even requested that they step down.

Roads along Monivong Boulevard and Commercial Boulevard were closed with military personnel. The police and military were there to crack down on this demonstration. Everywhere, starting from the Cambodian-Japanese Friendship Bridge across Monivong Boulevard to Eighteen March School ("sala dop pram bey mina" in Khmer), was full of military and police carrying AK-47 automatic riffles and ammunition. One could hear them shooting directly and indirectly at the student demonstrators as well as in the air.

I do not remember how many students were killed and how many were injured, but there were a lot.

Mom advised me not to participate in this demonstration. "If they can catch you, you will stay in prison for the rest of your life. Then you will have turned your life into a meaningless event." I definitely paid attention to mom's good advice and did not to walk in the street. I knew that the military and police might arrest me if I walked on the street, even if I were not a demonstrator.

I had to stay away from all political activity just to be on the safe side.

It was fine with me. Apart from working, I was doing my best at studying to take the university entrance exam again. I enrolled in the law school preparation class. I had an exam with the English Faculty and the Law School. At that time the Australian Quaker Services (QSA) ran the English Faculty. Most of the students knew that there would not be any corruption involved with any exam into the English Faculty.

Of course I finally did the exam, not only for the English faculty but also to the Law School.

I was so excited to hear the results. Each name of the students who passed the exam was announced. I was nervous and a little sad because I did not hear my name. Before the announcement ended, I heard my name, "Collacot" over the loudspeaker. Then I started jumping and shouting, "Yes! Yes! Finally, with God's help, I made it!"

The class started within two weeks of the announcement. I couldn't wait to attend my first year English class at the English Faculty of Phnom Penh University. As time passed I studied English there for more than 3 months. We had both an Australian English Teacher and a Cambodian Teacher who had lived in Australia and been naturalized to become an Australian citizen.

One day the Australian English Teacher announced that those who already knew some English could take a test and if they qualified, they could study in the year two classes instead of year one.

One month later, I heard from my friend that they saw my name on the passing list of students who would be allowed to study in the law school. I could not believe it. I rode my motorcycle to the law school so that I could see for myself. It was true! I saw my name, there.

I was so happy and said again, "My dream has come true. Thank God for his grace and mercy in helping me." I wanted to study in both faculties, but that was impossible because I was working as well as studying at the same time.

I decided to quite the English Faculty as a second year student and go to the Law School as a first year student. I believed my life to have new meaning.

I continued to use my little knowledge of English to teach the first session for new beginners, using Essential English Book One, from 11:30 a.m.-12:30 p.m., the second session with Essential English Book Two, from 12:30 p.m.-1:30 p.m. and in the evening the first session for new beginners, using Essential English Book One, from 5:30 p.m.-6:30 p.m. and the second session using Essential English Book Two, from 6:30 p.m.-7: 30 p.m. Therefore, I was teaching four hours a day.

I also continued to conduct my job search. Finally, I was invited for an interview with the Head of QSA, Mr. Mark. After the interview he got me a job working for the organization as a Teacher Assistant and Librarian. My job was to assist the Australian teachers in preparation with their teaching materials and lessons. I also worked as the librarian assisting students. I did this at QSA for one year.

Later, I became aware of a new opportunity to work for the UNAMIC and UNTAC as an interpreter and translator. This would help me to have more income for my family. I first got a job in the procurement and administration office. Then, I was transferred to the United Nations Mixed Military Working Group (MMWG) in the Force Commander Office, a high profile environment. When the United Nations Mission was first established, the military force commander was led by the French commander and then later by the Australian General John Sanderson.

There were four interpreters and translators in the MMWG, Force Commander Office. Ms. Dina was the first interpreter and translator for General John Sanderson. Mr. Mardi, was the second, I was the third, Mr. Oum Chanbot, the fourth, and if needed, Mr. Chivorn, a Cambodian Medical Doctor, was the fifth.

I was assigned to work with the State of Cambodia National Treasury, the Ministry of National Defense, Interior and Information. My job was to interpret at the round table meeting discussions and accompany United Nations Senior Military Officials to each Ministry during their visit. I also did translations of political documents, letters and correspondence.

As an interpreter and translator in the force commander's office, there were lots of opportunities for me to meet with all four of the Cambodian political party representatives. I always wanted to meet each one of them.

I was very curious to know many things: What do they look like? What is their character? How do they talk? What is their style of walking? Their heart? Are they an educated person with high moral? Do they know what is right and what is wrong? Who ordered the killing, and on and on. Especially, I wanted to meet personally the Prince and the Khmer Rouge Representative just for a second.

If I had a chance to meet them in person, I would ask why the Khmer Rouge Top Leaders like Brother number one, Pol Pot, Ieng Sary, brother number two, Nuon Chea, Son Sen, Ta Mok, Kiev Samphan and all other of their top Senior Military Commanders had accomplished in participation in the order to kill millions of my own people. One can see the dead were piled up like mountains.

Does this show that you all, the Khmer Rouge Top Leaders, love your own country, people and society. Khmer Rouge moved Cambodia at least fifty year back in development as equal as the

Sangkum Reas Niyum, King Sihanouk Regime. During the Khmer Rouge, we lost all our dignity, value, culture, morale and everything. Base people and new people who were from elsewhere were like wild animals to each other because of the evil teaching of Angkar, evil communist.

Khmer Rouge Top Leaders like Brother number one, Pol Pot, Ieng Sary, brother number two, Nuon Chea, Son Sen, Ta Mok, Kiev Samphan and all others of their top Senior Military Officials knew that they had done many bad things- massacred their own people, they did not allow people to have enough food to eat, they separated children from parents, husbands from wives, grandmothers from grand fathers, they forced people to work 20 hours a day, developed hatred and on and on. Therefore, they had the fear of reaction and revenge toward them.

This fear developed in the mindset of the Khmer Rouge top leaders- Brother number one, Pol Pot, Ieng Sary, brother number two, Nuon Chea, Son Sen, Ta Mok, Kiev Samphan, and all other top local military cammanders participated in this crime and all other of their top Senior Officials, every innocent person who said Angkar does not do the right thing was considered the enemy of their revolution. So now, all the new people were their enemy. After they killed the new people, city base people who were from the city. Then they started killing the base people, countryside base people who used to support them in their revolution. Then their own members of accusing them that they were the spy, the CIA for U.S and western imperialist and secret services of Vietnamese government.

Finally, everyone, the entire population in the country was his or her enemy. The enemy of their revolution. Then they just killed and killed their own people. Now everybody was their enemy, which included their long-lost comrade in arms, holding minister post in their own Khmer Rouge regime, Mr. Hou Yun, Mr. Hou Nim, Khmer Rouge Party Secretary, Mr. So Phim, Mr. Koy Thoun, Mr. Vorn Vet, Mr. Chau Seng former prime minister in the old regime who used to support their revolution, and intellectuals and scientists were killed because of the accusation that they were the enemy of the revolution.

Brother number one, Pol Pot, Ieng Sary, brother number two, Nuon Chea, brother number three, Son Sen, Defense Minister, Ta Mok, Military Regional Commander, Kiev Samphan, head of state and all other of their top Senior Officials did not tell the exact place where they lived and where they eat, where they went and where they worked and where their offices were because of the fear of a plot against them.

These Khmer Rouge Top Leaders- Brother number one, Pol Pot, Ieng Sary, brother number two, Nuon Chea, brother number three, Son Sen, Defense Minister, Ta Mok, Military Regional Commander, Kiev Samphan, head of state and all other of their top Senior Officials claimed that they loved Cambodia, nation and people but in reality they were not. They all were given an order to kill their own people.

I still did not understand what they said because it was completely different from their actions-killing, tyrannizing, separating, forcing people to do hard labor until collapse, no food to eat, close out schools, markets, hospitals, places to worship, churches, temples and on and on. How can you stand as a giant country if you are not united as one? Like the Khmer saying, "one chop stick, one can break easily but if we unite and combine together, no body can break us". This showed that when there was unity and solidarity within a nation, other nations couldn't do anything about it.

Didn't they see their government in poverty and hunger killed their own people. Their philosophy said, they tried to make society equal with no classes. They already knew that every society has classes even their own regime.

Their idea was completely different from Hitler's. Hitler killed other nations to dominate the world. Hitler's idea was that Germany was the only superior and divine nation on earth.

One day, as an interpreter and translator, I was asked to greet the Khmer Rouge representative, did not recall but probably by the name of Tep Konal, late 40, Chan You Ran, late 50 and others to Supreme National Council which is located Force Commander office, UNTAC Head Quarter.

I greeted them and said, "How do you do, your Excellency" and asked them to take a seat. In my mind, I think gee, this is the representative to the Khmer rouge, the bloodshed and most evil regime, and a regime who killed their own people and destroyed their nation and country look like this. I begin having a conversation with their junior representatives, did not recall but probably by the name of Tep Konal and two others. I can read their mind that they were not allowed to talk. They just look at one another. This it remind me about my parents' word: " plan Kor Tree " in Khmer "Dam Doeum Kor" what they mean was to survive, close your mouths, pretend you did not see and know anything, don't ask, don't answer, if ask answer short then close your mouth again. They all look tough and full of evil in side their mind.

I finally did see Buddhist Liberal Democratic Party (BLDP) top representative, led by former Prime Minister Son San and his deputy Mr. Ieng Mouly, The National United Front for an Independent, Neutral, Peaceful, and Cooperative FUNCINPEC, headed by King Sihanouk and his deputy Prince Norodom Ranaridth and their other representative.

Woooo, I saw former Prime Minister Son San. He is tall with soft slow voice, calm and well-educated person and a nice man. Based on his character, I can say that he is a man of integrity who knows what is right and what is wrong. He is a man who can stand with the heat. He also has the capacity and suitable to be a leader. He is Khmer Krom. Khmer Krom means Cambodian who lives in Kampuchea Krom. Now, it's known as South Vietnam. He looks like my Grand father, Konh Yiep. My grand father knew him when they were small living in Kampuchea Krom together, our land but now the Vietnamese invasion and took our land with the French Governor cutting our land and gave it to them.

His deputy Mr. Ieng Mouly seems to me that he is a simple man. I did not know much about him.

Wooooooooo, again, I also saw Prince Norodom Ranaridth. He is as tall as myself around 5 foot and 5 feet (5"5'). This kind of height is considered OK in Cambodia. Based on what I see, I can say that he is also a well-educated person, nice but different from former Prime Minister Son San in character and the way he talks and walks. Prince to me, he is a nice person. But he probably cannot stand with heat because he used to have an easy life-style.

For Khmer Rouge Representatives, I can meet only their junior representatives. To me, the Khmer Rouge representatives, it seem like they are hiding something behind. They did not talk. They always have plain faces. I can tell that they are afraid of one another. I know exactly the same but kind of hard to express in English.

Mr. Kiev Samphan, and Mr. Son Sen were the senior representatives in the Supreme National Council (SNC). Pol Pot, Ieng Sary and Noun Chea sent their junior representative to the SNC first to see the reaction of the Mr. Hun Sen Government and the local people first before their top senior representative arrived.

This kind of fact finding mission for them first and these junior representatives had to report to their boss, which is the top khmer rouge leaders, Pol Pot, Ieng Sary that everything is ok before Pol Pot, brother number one and Ieng Sary, brother number two can send their top representatives here.

In my point of view, even though, Pol Pot has declared his resignation from the top position of Khmer Rouge but it seemed to me that he was still had all the powers between 1979 to early 1990. But later, the power was autonomous to each Khmer rouge military top leader region. The power now was with the war Lord who controled in each region of the country. For example, Ta Mok was the most powerful in Ang Long Veng region, near the Thai Border. I think these top war Lord have to have their good relationship and they have to reported to Pol Pot, Ieng Sary, Son Sen and Noun Chea or Kiev Samphan or unidentified power person.

I do not recall that either it was either Tuesday or Wednesday, when the Khmer Rouge top representative, Mr. Kiev Samphan, who used to be close to King Sihanouk during the war and Son Sen, Khmer Rouge Defense Minister arrived in Phnom Penh, Pochengton International Airport through the Thai Airway, flight originally from Bangkok, Thailand.

Ms. Dina who was the first interpreter and translator for Force Commander Office, the United Nations (UNTAC) General John Sanderson who was head of the mission advised her to first make an appointment for either for him or his deputy to meet Mr. Kiev Samphan and Mr. Son Sen a day a head before their arrival. The appointment was in the afternoon and it was confirmed by Khmer Rouge resident representative office. They both will stay in the villa, around 600 meters from East German Embassy.

Either General John Sanderson or his deputy with other UN senior official will meet them both in their villa of resident after they arrived from the airport.

Absolutely, there were hundreds of angry people whose families had died by the Khmer Rouge's, the journalists; the photographers and etc. were waiting Mr. Kiev Samphan and Mr. Son Sen at the airport. In side the crowd, there were secret services of the Mr. Hun Sen Government disguised as normal civilians.

After getting off the plane, Mr. Kiev Samphan and Mr. Son Sen was accompanied by their body guards and government police to put them both into the vehicle and drove by a government driver to the Khmer Rouge Villa of Resident, near the East German embassy.

They both were followed by the angry mobs from the airport to their Villa of Resident. Mr. Son Sen was not known in public. The mobs knew only Mr. Kiev Samphan. After the vehicle was stopped in front of their Villa of Resident to enter the villa entrance.

There were crowded surrounding everywhere. One can see taxi motorcycle drivers, cyclos drivers and people everywhere to surround the resident of Khmer rouge. The vehicle stopped cannot move because of the crowd.

Some of their bodyguards tried to stop the angry crowd to approach them. The others open the door for them to get out. Either Mr. Kiev Samphan or Mr. Son Sen told their bodyguards not to use the AK 47 rifle to shoot in the open air and threaten the crowd. They both wanted to proceed by peaceful means.

They can stop the anger mobs by using AK 47 riffle to open fired into the air but they didn't. The solution was a good too.

Some of the crowd shouted to them both " you killed my parents, now give their life back to me", others said "you killed my sister and brother, now give their life back to me" continued " you killed my whole family, you caused me to live in the orphanage and let me grow-up without seeing my father and mother and having a bad life and miserable life, now you give all back to me, continued " you are evil, you killed my whole family and Khmer people" how foolish were you to do so? Now you give me back. Some continued, " What 's your problem? Why do you order to kill many innocent people? Didn't you see human life was important and nothing to compare? Why you did that, now you give me back and continued on and so.

Finally, the situation was in chaos. No body could control the situation only the government police, but they did not interfered. The government was the only force that can control the situation but they didn't. They let it go. They closed their eyes and open another just to see.

In my point of view, this was an arrangement as well. The police forces might got an order from the top government leader not to interfered, just watch and see but do not let the crowd hit them until they both died. Just let them having serious injury because of the blown of the crowd, that would be enough. So that, we did not get blamed from the national and international press.

It was absolutely true. Mr. Kiev Samphan was hit by unidentified angry mobs in many places in his body and especially, the head and his blood was blown everywhere. His head was full of blood. I stood there around 200 meters from the crowd, I can see, he took his both hand to stop and covered the blood from running out of his head.

For Mr. Son Sen, I think he got hit just a few but not serious like Mr. Kiev Samphan.

Seeing that now the situation worsened, if they let the blood continued to flown out from the Mr. Kiev Samphan's head, he might die. Therefore, the government police force moved in their military armor personnel, made in the former Soviet Union quickly and took them both in the armor and drove them back to Pochengton International Airport back to Bangkok, Thailand.

After the incident happened, most of Cambodian good and innocent families were spreading out the rumor that the unidentified persons that hit Mr. Kiev Samphan in the head was the Vietnamese secret services with the cooperation of the Government police forces collaboration.

Most Cambodian people like me, thought that it could be true too or it might not be the Vietnamese intelligence at all but that was an arrangement, it's absolutely true. Even though, my father, five uncles, three aunts and five cousins had died by Pol Potist's, I didn't dare to use my anger to attack the Khmer Rouge leaders because the government, regime, can bring you to justice, if you dare to do so.

On another hand, they can accuse you of being a person who stop the peace process and national reconciliation between Khmer and Khmer. They could bring you to life sentence.

Therefore, in my point of view, nobody dare to do so. This was organized by the secret service of the government with the cooperation of the Vietnamese intelligence inside Cambodia.

At this time, I did not recall because I was not on official duty that day. I heard from my friend that Ms. Dina who was the first interpreter and translator for Force Commander Office, the United Nations (UNTAC) Official with the driver and the United Nations Representative in the vehicles that stop by 500 meters from the Villa of Khmer Rouge Resident, near East German Embassy saw the unrest situation like this decided to return to the (UNTAC) HQ and told what was happened when arriving at the HQ.

This year was the year that I just started to come to know the world. I dreamed of flying the plane and having my own car. Through, my job as an interpreter and translator, I traveled by the United Nations military helicopters and plane-C160 and C130. When it landed in each region, we got a Japanese made vehicle, Land cruiser with the United Nations licensed plate and sign use as our daily transportation.

Now, I had a chance to visit difference provinces-Kampong Som, Kampot, Siem Reap, Kampong Chhnang, Kampong Speu, Kandal, Takeo, Battambang and other western parts of the country. When arriving in each province, I can see the achievements-buildings, roads, small power plants, electricity milestones, parks and so on of the previous regime left behind.

This indication that the old regime was so developed in that time compared to now there was nothing that had been done. One can see things that destroyed but not done. So sad to see all of that.

I felt so excited to have a test drive this vehicle with the advice and the direction from the United Nations Drivers. Finally, I learned how to drive the vehicle.

Most of my neighbors now, they are kind of praising myself because they see that I am now some body. They cannot do what they want to my family any longer. They cannot abuse their power to my family any more.

I sometimes, bring in the United Nations Representatives to visit my apartment just let **them** know that I am now some body. You cannot treat me badly **as** you did 6 or 8 years ago. Now, I am a grown young man with resources.

Every time, they see me, they used nice words with me. That this does not happened before. I forgave and forgot them about what they did to my family as God's word. Some had died because of their sin and disease.

In Cambodia, the simple people never have a chance to fly the plane. Only rich people that can seat on or flying a plane!

This year was a year of joy, a year of happiness within the family. Our family had plenty of food to eat. I can eat what I want. My family living condition was much better than before especially from 1981 to early 1990. When the United Nations established its mission in Cambodia, I started seeing the glimpse of light to fulfill my dream. In my mind, heart and soul, there will not be long, what ever I have planned and wanted and dreamed for which including my strong desire to have a good life will be fulfilled one day at a time.

The State of Cambodia (SOC) 1991-1992
My Life to the Glimpse and Sunrise

I was a Buddhist since birth. It was inherited from my parents, grand parents and great grand parents. But I do not know why, I always want to be a Christian Protestant and get marry at the Christian Church since I was a young. I dreamed of having a good, tough, family-oriented and light skin wife.

This year was a year that I met a group of Christian evangelists, Phnom Penh Church of Christ, Baptist Church, by the name of Mark, a young pastor from America and his congregation. Pastor Mark was in a small apartment along Angdoung Road and USSR BOULEVARD established this Christian church. He and his group preached good news and shared gospel with me and all other Khmer, young men and women. At first, we just wanted to make friend with foreigners to practice our English language. We're Buddhist. It is hard to convert our believes to Christianity because our great grand parents and parents were Buddhist.

Every Sunday and Thursday, we all met at Phnom Penh Church of Christ. We started bible study and getting to know church members, evangelists from America, Singapore and the Philippine. Within a couple of months, pastor Mark and his group arranged us for baptism in Chaktomok River, in front of the Royal Palace. Before the baptism, Pastor Mark asked us to confess our sins to him. Each one of us have to confess what we have done wrong during the past.

(blank)

So quick, first, my turn came up and I did not know what to say. I started asking him questions, why I have to tell him. I continued, I do suppose to confess my sins directly to God, Jesus Christ, don't I?

He said yes, to him. He asked me to lists all things that I have done wrong and I have to tell in front of him, personally. I started tell him honestly. First, I told him that I am a good person. I never cheat and doing bad things to anyone, hardly lie and false statement. I did lot of good deed, kindness and helpful to every person especially the elders and the needy.

My parents taught me since birth that " honesty and kindness will never die ". If you help one people, one day someone will help you back. It might not be that person but there will be help.

The bad things were I steal food, fruits and anything that is eatable to eat and lies to survive during the Khmer Rouge, communist regime. If you did not steal during the Khmer Rouge, you would be dead because of hunger, starvation and hard labor in the concentration camp. The food rations that the high organization known as "Angkar", an evil communist provided us was not enough to eat. During the Khmer Rouge, Bloodshed regime, we, Cambodian never satitiated with food.

One day, when my mother visit village from her mobile concentration camp, I brought her to collective community to have food, there where Angkar arranged food for all villagers. I had already had one in that evening but the food ration was very small with full of rice porridge liquid and it was not enough to me. But I disguised that I did not have food yet. Therefore, my mother and I have to line up again. Finally, Khmer Rouge Officer noticed me that I had already had food but not my mother. Then the Khmer Rouge with a strong punishment caught me.

I continued since the Khmer Rouge regime collapsed, I never did bad things again.

Pastor Mark started asking me again, what did you used to do? I said nothing. I asked him in return if God, Jesus Christ has a divine revelation and power, why He did not help our people when He see the pain, suffering, needy, starvation and hunger and the killing of innocent people during Khmer Rouge regime. How come and where is God let them kill these innocent, good people? Where is Him? Why He didn't perform His miracle to help them out and where is God during a time like this. Their death was piled up like mountain.

Pastor Mark answered, "No One Know about God's Will and Purpose".

Then, my turn is finished and he turned up to the next one.

When all the young men and women have finished confession their sins before pastor Mark, then we all drove our bicycles and motorcycles to the riverside to do baptism that evening.

To be honest, I did not know deeply what is baptism mean during that time. What I though was to wash and clean up my sins that full of dirtiness to be a cleaned cut person.

I do not know why I always want to get marriage in the Church. All my siblings, there is only me who had become a new creature, new born to be a Christian, protestant. My brothers and sisters said, why I stop worship Buddhist's God. They continued Buddhist teach us to do good deed to all people, not to steal, to kill, to lie but to be a good person. I told him in return, have you seen any Buddhist and Islamist help people in refugee camp or any place around the world???

Through my search to know who is the living God whom He always protect and save me during the Khmer Rouge (KR) and the People's Republic of Kampuchea (PRK), these two communist regime, is our Almighty God, Jesus Christ. I always do meditation and prayer, asked God, Christ Jesus to give me guidance and direction. Then, he always gives me clear, true vision and sign before things happened and with Him, I will have eternal life. Finally, I accepted the Lord my God, Jesus Christ as my Lord and Savior and I put my faith in Him since then.

Sometimes, I went to worship the Lord through the invitation of a Singaporean woman who live and work in Phnom Penh at the resident of World Vision International. There, during the morning worship and prayer, I saw lot of people who is foreign believers from eastern and western countries working and living in Cambodia, crying, crying, speaking in tongue, shouting "Halleluiah, Halleluiah along with clapping their hand, dancing and jumping and said Amen and on and on". Then I started feeling uncomfortable and nervous. I started looking around again and again and wonder their strange behavior and action during this prayer time.

A Buddhist person, when you worship, pray and meditate Buddha, you do in a quiet with peaceful mind. You speak to him quietly in your mind that no one can hear.

I talked to myself; these foreigners probably have mental and psychological problems. I started asking myself again and again, why these people have mental and psychological matters. I saw them as a decent and good people before the worship and prayer time came. Why they have this kind of disease?

That morning, I left the worship place, resident of world vision international with a series of questions and wondering in my mind why these people have difference characters, behavior and action while they were praying.

Now, Pastor Mark has asked me to stop working for the United Nations Advance Mission in Cambodia (UNAMIC) and requested me to working and serving the Lord, Jesus Christ. I told Pastor Mark that it was my honor to serve the Lord but I have to feed my family and my self first. I was taught that help yourself and your family first before   God can help you. Therefore, I am unable to work for the Lord every day as pastor Mark's suggestion. I told pastor Mark that I am willing to work for God if he can give me some kind of compensation in return to feed my family and myself. He continued that your job and responsibility is to wide-spreading the good news, share gospel with people and encourage them to accept Jesus Christ and become a newly born to be a Christian. Pastor Mark got angry with me because the only thing I could accept his proposal is that my family and I need to live as well.

This year after office and school hours, I involved with Christian Ministry. I am mostly at the church. Therefore, my family was kind of unhappy with my decision. They said, I did not have time to help our family out.

I always give thanks to our Almighty God, Jesus Christ that He always with me and give me direction and guidance in a good and bad time.

This year was a happiest year in my life to see now, the United Nations has set up peace accord and asked all parties involved to cease fired and completed foreign troops, Vietnamese withdrawal from Cambodia. There is a glimpse of light from the horizon has come for not only this nation but also my family and myself. All of our people including myself hope that now it is time for all Cambodian to be in one accord and its leaders to rebuild the country.

All of Cambodian including myself wants to see our country as progress as Singapore, Japan, the United States of America, Australia, France, and England and like other western countries. A glimpse of light has come to Cambodia again after thirty years of war. The first step of the progress was peace and stability has come. It is now a time for Cambodia and her people to learn about the past and take that experiences to make this country happened toward hope, joy, harmony, well being, prosperity and especially happiness for the entire country.

This year was the year that there was many foreign investors started investing and doing businesses in the Kingdom of Cambodia like the saying said, "the early birds catch its worm". What I mean was since there was no competition; the first businesses are normally make high profit and having mutual benefits for all parties. One can see roads and bridges was rebuild that can link the entire country together. Hotel, guest house, high building, power plantation, water and sewage supplies, manufactures of all kind, telecommunications is growing like mushroom in rainy season. This was the first time that this country open to the rest of the world after many years of war. I also have an opportunity to contribute in rebuilding my own country as well.

With the opportunity to working with the United Nations, I met Trishatur Lagalia and Lucy Abbot on their first arrival working with the United Nations Transitional Authority in Cambodia (UNTAC). They both are New Yorker, working in the Procurement Unit under the Administration Division.

Within the United Nations, I'm first working for Procurement Unit later with Mixed Military Working Group (MMWG) under the UN Force Commander Office. Trish is my supervisor and later we both become friend till now.

This year, we, Trish, Phannarith, Lucy, Mony and myself have an opportunity to visit Bangkok, Thailand by the UN military plane C-160. The plane was landing in Bangkok International Airport; all the UN staffs including myself were outboard from the plane.

Trish, Phannarith, Lucy, Mony and I passed Thai immigration, and then we all took a taxi to Ambassador Hotel, which is located in the heart of Bangkok, Thailand. I was so excited to see Bangkok. Bangkok, Thailand. I said to myself, gee, Bangkok is so developed with skyscraper and good road and highway that can link to their entire cities and country. I was kind of amaze to see the leadership of this country.

Then I started questions, myself and our country leadership was not smart and intelligent like other countries in South East Asia. Why, we were always in war between Khmer and Khmer because of first the pressure proxy war between the east (communist) and west (capitalist) ideology, second selfishness of individual who are greedy and want power. This kind of person can do everything to please his foreign master who support him to be in the power for the rest of their live. In return, this leader have to commit and done anything that their foreign master asked for. The only solution is to teach individual to have an education, understand the value the love of God and the love of mankind toward one another with people, community and country interest as a whole. When we will have truly peace, stability, prosperity and happiness in the Khmer family as well as in the whole country.

Phannarith, Mony and I were very happy to visit Thailand. We all stayed in Bangkok for a couple of days then we traveled to Pataya Resources. This is the first time that we all came to see the world. We were amazed to learn and see something new in Thailand especially skyscraper, escalator and elevator in the Malls and hotels and everything.

Phanarith and I stayed in the same room in the hotel. It was funny and lack of knowledge, what we thought was the total cost of our stay in hotel was already including in the room booking which we were paid in advance. Therefore, we both started drinking all the soft drink and wines in refrigerator in the hotel where we stayed.

This was the great experience that we, Phanarith, Mony and I came to see the world. We also had an opportunity to stop by at the United Nations Office in Bangkok as well. Upon our returned to Phnom Penh, Cambodia, we all felt so excited with happiness to see the great development of our neighboring countries like Thailand. We walked off from the ramp stair of an airplane like we were from another well planet on earth.

We all hope that one day, we will have an opportunity to become Cambodian top leaders so that we can lead our country toward security, peaceful, development, growth, harmony, prosperity and happiness.

And there were a Cambodian saying "Good leaders lead the country toward peaceful, harmony and prosperity" on the other hand evil leaders, like Pol Pot, Ieng Sary and Khiev Samphan lead the country toward poverty, consequent and harm ness. We can compare leaders as vehicle's driver. No matter what kind of good vehicle you have, if you are a bad driver with lack of knowledge, love, godly human heart in your mind, heart and soul you will let your vehicle being out of order or problem.

The Kingdom of Cambodia (KOC) 1992-1993
My Life in the Glimpse and Sunrise

1992-93 was the year that civil war and the proxy war between communist and capitalist ideology ended. Peace came to Cambodia and the world with the help of the United States Government during the presidencies of Ronald Reagan and George H. W. Bush and the United Nations. For the first time in forty years there was no open conflict.

The country's name was again made the Kingdom of Cambodia. Free and fair general elections were held with the support of the United Nations and the U.S Government. A new chapter opened for the country and her people. Christian evangelists came to Cambodia and Christian churches grew up everywhere over the entire country.

The Cambodian people started having hope that peace, prosperity and happiness were possible for this nation. We decided that we had to forget and learned about the past while at the same time learning from our experiences so that we did not make the same mistakes again.

Our experience with communism was terrible. Its purpose seemed to be to threaten, to starve, to murder and to brutalize our own people. - Pol Pot of Cambodia was like Hitler of Germany, Stalin of the former Soviet Union and Mao Tse Tong of China. They did awful things to their own people. This evil communist leadership affected many people around the world.

But in all circumstances in every society and country, God always places good people He can use. The United States Presidents Ronald Reagan and George H.W Bush as well as the former Soviet Union Premier Mikhail Gorbachev are good examples. They helped to bring about the end of communism not only in the world but also in Cambodia and peace for the country in 1992. I believe this was evidence of the power of our Almighty God, Jesus Christ helping from behind the scenes.

I quote the two presidents' words, "Never before has the idea that peace is indivisible been so true as it is now. Peace is not unity in similarity but unity in diversity, in the comparison and conciliation of differences. In our times, good relations benefit all. Any worsening of relations anywhere is a common loss."

These presidents have Godly characteristics, charisma and values in common--peace, freedom, democracy, human rights and prosperity to all mankind. I quote the words of Premier Mikhail Gorbachev, "In the name of Communism we abandoned basic human values. So when I came to power in Russia, I started to restore those values; values of "openness" and freedom".

God always has His people to continue the work even though they may have to face many difficulties, suffering, lost and other tribulations but stand firm in the time like this. For example after President Ronald Reagan paved the way for the next president to carry on and the process of bringing peace, stability and the world together, God, Christ Jesus has His other people like Vice President, George H. W. Bush. God made him to be the President of the United States through democracy and with His invisible help.

I quote once again the words of these Godly presidents – Reagan, Bush and Gorbachev, which they said together during Premier Mikhail Gorbachev's official visit to the United States, in New York, "We are witnessing most a profound social change."

Through my life experience, I believe that when a person is born, our Almighty God, Jesus Christ already has prepared his or her book of life. This book has recorded all circumstances and events in their life, what they have to go through, what will happen, and how each individual life will be ended.

The dream, vision and passion of each individual will play a major role in their life. We have to do our best in all circumstances – good times and bad times--and leave the rest with Almighty God, Jesus Christ.

Dreams, visions and passion create the master plan of our life. To reach our goal, we have to firstly accept our Almighty God, Jesus Christ into our heart and soul as our Lord and Savior. I did this when I converted from Buddhist to Christianity. I believe Christianity is the only hope for salvation. We Christians depend only on Him along with working very hard and staying positive with our plans, no matter what we go through in life. We must stand firm, live with integrity, morality, fairness, honesty, generosity, love, helping one another and stay positive at all times. We have to give thanks to Him in every circumstances. These key values will never die not only in Christianity but also in any environment.

When we have our Almighty God, Jesus Christ in our heart and soul, based on the scripture we can say, "I can do everything through Christ who strengthens me." If what we do is according to His will, we will be able to achieve everything. If not, we are not going to be successful.

I was born in a middle class family. My family, in fact all of the Cambodian people and I have gone through similarities in life with the most evil Khmer Rouge Communist and then the People's Republic of Kampuchea (PRK) is the better than the KR. These were evil communist regimes.

It was very difficult to convert my beliefs from Buddhism into Christianity. But everything with God, Jesus Christ is possible. He will open the way for us through our daily life experience to accept Him, Jesus Christ as our Lord and Savior.

173

My great-grand parents, grandparents and parents were Buddhist. I was a Buddhist for twenty-one years. I was also taught about Buddhism all of my life. I do not understand why I always wished to be a Christian protestant and married as a Christian in a church.

If you are a Buddhist, you are not allowed to marry in church. It is against your beliefs. Therefore, I decided to get involved with church. I started attending Bible study and Sunday services.

I also started looking back on the life that I had gone through during these two evil communist regimes- Khmer Rouge and the People's Republic of Kampuchea (PRK). There were always, not only good people from other people within the communist regimes, something to help me survive. Sometimes also supernatural events – like the fall of fruit from a palm tree on militiamen's head, which made them unconscious and created an opportunity for me to escape. This was a true miracles.

Finally, it was time for me to decide and be baptized. I was baptized in Chatomouk River, in front of the Royal Palace, Phnom Penh, the capital of the Kingdom of Cambodia.

As a newly born, I knew nothing about Christianity. I looked on mature Christians and compared myself to them. I started judging them. This was completely wrong. As a Christian what we have to do is to look on our Almighty God, Jesus Christ.

In every aspect of life and in everything I do, no matter small or big, I have to do my best along with prayer and ask my Almighty God, Jesus Christ for guidance and direction. Then He will show us the way and the solution to make our decisions to reach our goal.

Because the power of prayer is the power that comes to us through our Almighty God, Jesus Christ, when we are in the midst of confusion and uncertainty in our daily lives. It's the power that comes to help us to have good and clear direction.

The power of prayer is the constant renewal of perspective. Prayer opens our heart, soul and eyes. It extends our horizons. It sheds light into the darkness of our fears, uncertainty, confusion, frustrations and our sorrows, our hopes, joys, our shame and our pride. It gives us new ways of seeing life and relationships, of understanding work and the cost of growing.

Prayer to God should be persistent with thanksgiving. Prayer is the only way of communication with our Almighty God, Jesus Christ. I can feel it and know it and depend on it. It comes to me as well as to other human beings as a gift, but we need to do our part and keep it alive all the time as well. Jesus calls us to pray and through our prayers, He empowers us and gives us strength and energy as He directs our ways toward solutions.

I always ask myself, first question was when will I be able to come to America and second, who will be my future wife. On my last year at the Law School, there was an inter governmental for higher educational exchange program between Cambodia Faculty of Law and Economic Sciences, French Universities, French Republic and American Universities, the United States of America. Every time, there was a representative from these western countries, my schoolfellow are always looking for me to do an interpretation for our associate dean of the Faculty. Thank God, Christ Jesus finally, I had an opportunity to come to America.

Now, God has answered my first question that I had been waiting for more than twenty years. I keep continue to challenge God on my second question.

One day, while living and studying in America, I was introduced by a woman name Leakhena whom I knew and I used to help her to get a job with Australian Telecommunication Company, Telstra OTC, to her relative, Romona who live in Texas. She is a Godly and beautiful woman.

We, Romona and I had a long distance relationship. First, I thought we just a friend. Our relationship has turned from days to months. Then from months to nearly year. She asked me to come and visit her in Texas. I told her that no, I do want to visit you in Texas because it was too hot there. Can you come over to Massachusetts? She said "If you do not want to come, we just friend."

She also had a persistence prayer to God if I am Mr. Right for her. In her prayer, she said if I do not come and live in Texas, then we just a friend. What it means is, it was not God's will for her.

I always prayer to God and ask Him to give me guidance and direction and some kind of sign through my dream and vision to identify that she will be Miss. Right for me, my future wife.

That day, the day I said no to her. I started having a strong and break through prayer. That night, God gave me a real sign with divine revelation. I saw her in my dream "she had a small piece of red cloth ties on her hand and also with that same small piece of red cloth ties on my hand as well." After that I said, yes, yes, that's the one. God had given me a clear divine revelation already. Then I decided to call her the next day that I am coming to Texas.

When I met her to first time, it seem that everything was not going well. But I still have confident on God. I talked to myself again and again that all things are possible with God's will. Just wait and see, how does it go. Finally, as time goes by, we had established a strong and healthy relationship. Then, I had an opportunity to marriage to a beautiful woman, Romona. We married at the Church of Champion. I was also waiting for thirty year to have God answer my prayer on my second question.

As the scripture said in the book of Jeremiah 29:11 "For I know the plans I have for you, declares the Lord, "plans to prosper you and not to harm you, plans to give you

Hope and a future." and Psalm 33:20-21 "We wait in hope for the Lord; He is our help and our shield. In Him our hearts rejoice, for we trust in his holy name. Yes! I have been waiting for more than twenty years to come to America and to have a future wife for thirty but finally, I did.

While we wait, God puts the pieces of our life's puzzle into place so that his ultimate desire for us will be fulfilled. Our waiting allows for his working. That's what we're waiting for-for God's work to be completed in our lives.

By looking back, my family's survival, including my Mom, brother Reagan, and sister Margaret and me, from the two evil communist regimes, Khmer Rouge (KR) and the People's Republic of Kampuchea (PRK) is because of our Almighty God, Jesus Christ is always with us in all circumstances and environments. He worked behind the scenes. He has a well designed plan that at the time of tribulation and crisis, we normal human beings cannot see.

But we also have to do our best in everything- trying harder, doing better, keep on going and maintain good relationship with Him in all times with persistence communication and prayer. When we have God, Jesus Christ in our heart and soul, we are on His vessel and the glimpse of light from the horizon will come and shine on each one of us in one day at a time.

Romona and I are living in peace, security, harmony, well-being and happiness under our All Mighty God, Christ Jesus Kingdom. There are many things we have to do- good deeds to everyone especially the elder, needy and the poor, widespread the good news, to share gospel, being His good servants and to have our own children to be our inheritance to continue our success journey in life with Him forever.

Printed in the United States
143070LV00002B/17/P